NEW DANCE
Approaches to Nonliteral Choreography

NEW DANCE

Approaches to Nonliteral Choreography

MARGERY J. TURNER

With RUTH GRAUERT
and ARLENE ZALLMAN

University of Pittsburgh Press

Published by the University of Pittsburgh Press, Pittsburgh, Pa. 15260
Copyright © 1971, University of Pittsburgh Press
All rights reserved
Manufactured in the United States of America

10 9 8 7 6 5 4 3

Library of Congress Catalog Card Number 74-134491
ISBN 0-8229-5269-6

The dance is in the dancer and the dancer is in
the dance. Where is the dance when no one is dancing
it? What man is a dancer except when he is dancing?

John Ciardi

Contents

Illustrations

Preface

The purpose of this book is to help reduce the broad gap that exists between significant new developments in the dance field and their dissemination to dance students in schools and colleges. This book, then, is intended for teachers and students.

The materials and methods presented here as tools in creating nonliteral dance are offered as suggestions, not as any kind of rigid system or inviolable set of standards. Based on my own knowledge of the movement medium and my experience with creative forms of art and education, the approaches detailed in this book are intended as a guide to both teacher and student. It is hoped that the individual will use the suggested procedures as a jumping-off point, supplementing them with his own experiences and perspectives.

This book is directed to students and teachers in public as well as professional schools. In both areas they should be concerned with providing artistic experiences, stimulating interest in dance, developing the student's ability to move effectively, and exploring the materials of dance. The only difference in their adaptation of these methods should be in the quantity of dance experience provided. Time limitations in nonprofessional schools can be met by reducing the size of the assignment, but inadequate class time should never result in a lowering of standards or a lessening of quality. By participating in aesthetically sound dance experiences, the student can transcend himself, discover his body as a highly effective means of communication, and explore fully the world of movement and imagination; he may do this for professional reasons or for no other reason than pure enjoyment and a healthy escape from reality.

Another advantage of the nonliteral approach to dance is its absence of emotion in its natural and dramatic forms. It should, therefore, be much more attractive to teachers who are embarrassed by working with emotionally charged material. The nonliteral approach lends itself well to the current emphasis in physical education on intensive study of movement exploration and motor learning; and by eliminating all emotional overtones, it diminishes the biggest barrier that has formerly existed in training of physical education teachers to teach dance.

Based on extensive research conducted over a two-year period at the Henry Street Playhouse School of Dance, this text also draws heavily on my observation and study of the work of other dance artists representing the second cycle of modern dance, as well as my own experimentation and teaching. I am especially grateful to Alwin Nikolais for his unending cooperation in my research and for providing the constant challenge that sent me in pursuit of a deeper understanding of the modern dance artists of today. His daring and innovative dance theater productions have opened many exciting areas for exploration.

I want to acknowledge the fine help of Arlene Zallman, a musician of unusual creative talent, in contributing the chapter on music for dance. Thanks go as well to Ruth Grauert, an outstanding artist in theatrical lighting for dance, for her chapter on dance lighting. I am also grateful to Nina Shoehalter for perceptive editing of my manuscript and to Kay Mollis for secretarial assistance.

Introduction

Since the beginnings of modern dance, experts have speculated and argued about the essentials of modern dance choreography. The ongoing controversy has produced as many theories as there are dancers and teachers.

The first forty years of modern dance development evolved around a core of established standards based on principles borrowed from other art forms. This search for fixed formulae led to a lengthy list of prescribed requirements essential for "good" choreography. Referred to as elements of dance, these requisites included such considerations as variety, contrast, balance, climax, sequence, transition, repetition, harmony, and unity. The preferences of dance artists and educators have varied widely from a random selection of some of these essentials to a strict insistence on the inclusion of all of them as indispensable to dance choreography. Since these requirements reflect principles borrowed from other art fields rather than those intrinsic to the movement medium, I believe it is risky to attribute absolute or final character to them unless they can be proven essential to choreography through thorough testing.

I recently attempted a research study in an effort to weigh the relative merits of choreographic structure and to identify essential elements of a movement theme in modern dance composition.[1] The

1. Margery J. Turner, "A Study of Modern Dance in Relation to Communication, Choreographic Structure, and Elements of Composition," *Research Quarterly of the American Association for Health, Physical Education and Recreation* 34, no. 2 (May 1963): 219–27.

results of my study showed that several of the traditional "elements" could be eliminated without impairing the whole; I concluded that the validity and indispensability of established essentials are highly questionable.

In order to build a firm philosophical foundation on which modern dance can grow and flourish, considerable study of choreographic ideas and values is needed. Such a foundation can evolve from study combining the extensive experiences of experimental dance artists and the empirical findings emerging from the dance research laboratory.

The pioneers in contemporary modern dance continue to discover new frontiers in their search for new expression. Since these innovators work intuitively, without regard for facts and findings, it is up to the dance researcher to supply the study and evaluations that are needed for the further development of dance. A person with extensive training and experience, the researcher should approach dance study free of personal bias or loyalty to any one school or point of view. Understanding both the artist and the needs of education, he must approach his task with the objectivity of a scientist and the sensitivity of an artist.

Unfortunately, there are too few dance researchers in the field. Dance teachers have tended to dismiss dance research because they reject the idea of measuring art. But they must be shown that there are many kinds of measurement and types of research other than statistical and quantitative evaluations. If educators and dance artists were to combine forces, applying their creative imagination to research design as well as to dance choreography, they could contribute significantly to the enrichment of the dance medium. Until such a collaboration is effected, dance research will have a long way to go to keep pace with the rapid changes the artists are making.

During the first half of this century, modern dance underwent many phases and forms. It moved from the free form period (adapted to education as natural dance) to the mechanistic phase with its rigidity, lack of imagination, and gross muscularity. The introspective and psychological phases were marked by emphasis on personal anguish, Freudian symbolism, and social consciousness.

Since the late 1940s, a second cycle of modern dance development has begun to emerge. Departing radically from the underlying traditional principles that served the first cycle, the new dance reflects the most recent technological developments in space, electronics, and the mass media. Its reliance on nonliteral choreography has meant the avoidance of the human emotional involvement that was so characteristic of the first cycle. Individuality is held supreme, as each artist seeks to discover dance for himself in terms of its basic materials and his own philosophical values.

During this same period a strong trend toward nonliteral choreography has been evident in ballet as well as in modern dance. This has resulted in a radical departure from ballet of previous periods. These changes are reflected most clearly in the works of George Balanchine and Robert Joffrey. Much of their choreography strongly resembles modern dance of the late forties. In contemporary ballet the story is all but extinct; even electronic music has found its way into the ballet world. This merging of forms has led to employment of some modern dance choreographers by ballet companies. The trend will probably continue to merge these two forms. One day we may refer to the various forms of dancing as simply *dance,* and identify the kind by the person producing it. The demands of musical comedy, as well as newer movements in various art forms, have also been influential in bringing about changes on the contemporary dance scene.

Unhappily, educational dance has not kept up with the exciting new directions in dance with their profusion of experimental styles. One reason for this cultural lag has been the notable slowness of educators to adapt to changes: many have had minimal training and infrequent exposure to recent trends because of geographical isolation from the dance centers. The gap is widened further by the dearth of people who are qualified to inform educators about the changing dance scene and by the financial limitations that prevent professional companies from traveling. Hopefully, the increasing availability of foundation and government matching grants will allow more dance companies to travel extensively.

One of the ways in which the cultural gap can be bridged is through the wider use of good dance films and written teachers' guides. Although high quality dance films are rare and at best cannot compare to a live dance performance, they can be valuable as an additional learning experience. If we are to bring dance education up to date, we must raise the money to meet the high cost of film production and conveniently located film libraries.

The lag can be further reduced by the employment of dance artists for teaching at the college level. Experience has shown that professional dancers as college teachers have created better understanding and acceptance of the radical, sophisticated departures typical of the new dance. With dance innovators working on their own campuses, colleges will be able to witness firsthand the significant new developments in contemporary dance.

NEW DANCE
Approaches to Nonliteral Choreography

The Nature of Nonliteral Dance

What Is Nonliteral Dance?

Nonliteral dance is the art of movement and motion.[1] Whereas other art forms do use some movement in their creative expression (such as motorized sculpture and moving constructions of painters), dance relies almost exclusively on movement and motion as the vehicles for communication.

As a nonverbal medium, dance concerns itself not with thoughts or ideas but with feelings, attitudes, images, relationships, shapes, and forms that can be communicated directly through the senses. Because of its noncerebral nature, dance relies for its coherence on a form of motor logic;[2] the dancers and choreographers proceed intuitively in evaluating and ordering their movements. In the process, movement combinations are either accepted or rejected because they "feel" right or wrong in a specific context.

Among the barriers to public understanding of the new dance is its unfamiliarity. Many are apprehensive over the notion that nonliteral dance is abstract, that it is removed from daily experience and therefore not immediately understandable. Yet this abstraction exists only in the perception of the inexperienced observer; to the

---

1. *Movement* is the fact of bodily action. *Motion* is the illusion and residual action resulting from the kind of movement produced.

2. *Logic* is here meant in the sense of the articulation and ordering of movement guided by neuromuscular skill and kinesthetic awareness; an intuitive sense of movement order.

dancer and choreographer, the materials of the movement medium are just as concrete and real as sounds are to a musician and colors and textures to a painter.

Just as contemporary music is sometimes considered dissonant and unpleasant to many because they are not open to listening for new sound relationships, so nonliteral modern dance is sometimes labeled as abstract because its movements are not traditional in form, style, or aesthetic values. If the spectator does not allow himself to respond to the unusual, new ways of moving, he is likely to regard the entire experience as out of focus and meaningless.

Besides the fact that the new dance is a young and rapidly developing art form, perhaps its major disadvantage is its limited exposure, both in terms of number of experiences and their duration. We can visit a gallery and study a painting for a long time; we can listen to recordings whenever and for as long as we wish. In other words, we can expose ourselves to other media both intensively and extensively. But we can experience a dance satisfactorily only when it is performed. While filmed recordings of dance performances can provide the opportunity for intensive study, their present state of imperfection means that they do not begin to capture the impact of the original or of live performance.

The Role of Illusion

Dance creates an aesthetic experience through a series of motional illusions. More than an arrangement of conceived and ordered movements,

the dance is an appearance, if you like, an apparition. It springs from what the dancers do, yet it is something else. In watching a dance you do not see what is physically before you—people running around or twisting their bodies; what you see is a display of interacting forces, by which the dance seems to be lifted, driven, drawn, closed or attenuated, whether it be solo or choric, whirling like the end of a dervish dance, or slow, centered and single in its motion. One human body may put the whole play of mysterious powers before you. But these powers, these forces that seem to operate in the dance, are not the physical forces of the dancer's muscles which actually cause the movements taking place. The forces we seem to perceive most directly and convincingly are created for our perception; and they exist only for it.[3]

Miss Langer suggests that the more perfect the dance, the less apparent are its actualities (muscularity, strength, control, etc.). What we experience, she says, are the elements artistically created; they are "the virtual realities—the moving forces of the dance, the apparent centers of power and their emanations, their conflicts and resolutions, lift and decline and their rhythmic life."[4] The aesthetic impact of the dance, then, lies in the totality of the illusion rather than in the parts that went into the creation of that illusion. The illusion exists for its own sake.

Meaning and Aesthetics in Nonliteral Dance

Nonliteral dance, communicating directly, needs no translation or explanation. It is a sensed experience whose value to the perceiver is determined by its overall impact on him. This impact is measured not only by the spectator's perceptive abilities, but also by the integrity of the dance itself. "The highest degree of expressiveness is attained when the artist has so treated each element in his work that its aesthetic meaning in relation to the whole appears to the competent spectator clear and unambiguous."[5]

Considerable confusion and disagreement center around exactly what is communicated and what a given contemporary dance work means. One cannot find traditional meaning—a specific message, lesson, or moral. This kind of meaning violates the basic premise of the art form—that art may exist for its own sake. If such meaning

3. Susanne Langer, "The Dynamic Image: Some Philosophical Reflections on Dance," *Dance Observer* 23, no. 6 (June–July 1956): 85–87.
4. Ibid.
5. Louis A. Reid, "Beauty and Significance," in *Reflections on Art*, ed. Susanne Langer (Baltimore: Johns Hopkins Press, 1958), p. 57.

exists, it probably results from the spectator's individual perception, from what he reads into the work.

Archibald MacLeish expresses this idea of a work of art existing for its own sake in "a poem should not mean, but be."[6] A dance should also *be*; its aesthetic value is in its very existence, in its creation of a movement-motion-space-time entity. Neither imitative nor representative, it is simply itself—a unified matrix of kinetically designed movement and motion.

Certainly not every dance, whether traditional or contemporary, can be considered an aesthetic expression. "Expression becomes aesthetic when it is carried out for the sake of its felt intrinsic value. If an expression, which at first was automatic, is repeated for the sake of the sheer joy of expression, at that point it becomes aesthetic."[7]

Aesthetic effectiveness is strongly related to clarity and unity—a kind of organic unity in which the dance work is disciplined to its form and content. Such unity results when the choreographer's sense of motor logic has operated on all phases of the choreographic process—conceiving, selecting, evaluating, refining, and relating the work to its source. "It is only when all of the factors of an image, all their individual effects, are completely attuned to the one intrinsic vital feeling that is expressed in the whole—when, so to speak, the clarity of the image coincides with the clarity of the inner content—that a truly artistic form is achieved."[8]

Dance by Chance

Merce Cunningham was the first choreographer to experiment with and produce dance-by-chance[9] procedures. Collaborating with

6. Archibald MacLeish, cited by Lucius Garvin, "The Paradox of Aesthetic Meaning" in *Reflections on Art*, p. 64.

7. Louis A. Reid, "Beauty and Significance," p. 53.

8. Paul Stern, "On the Problem of Artistic Form," in *Reflections on Art*, p. 75.

9. See Developing Movement Sequences in chapter 3.

John Cage, a musical experimenter and inventor of sound, and artist Robert Rauschenberg, Cunningham has had varying degress of success in experiments with choreographic processes involving chance. The aim of chance choreography or "indeterminacy," as John Cage calls it, is to achieve greater objectivity and freedom of exploration by eliminating the artist's personal values and tastes. As stated by Cage, "the field of awareness that's now open to us is so big that if we are not careful we'll just go into certain points in it, points with which we are already familiar. By using chance operations, we can get to points with which we are unfamiliar."[10] After all, the "great ideas which are landmarks in science have tended to be those which give us new orderings of facts previously unrelated, new and more comprehensive organizations of knowledge."[11]

Because one can never completely eliminate the processes of judgment and selection, however, dance by chance can never really be as indeterminate as it strives to be. Even when a coin is tossed to select movement, or to determine the order of movements, the fact remains that the choreographer will, through practice and conditioning, articulate those movements with some kind of motivation, even if it is based on intuition of motor sense. Individual differences are sharply evident, too, when one compares the chance work of an amateur with one choreographed by a professional. It would appear impossible then to eliminate such individual factors as training and skill.

Chance choreography is not merely a group free-for-all. It does involve some structuring. In fact it is really not so far removed from group choreography based on structured and practiced improvisation—a procedure that has been in use for a long time. Obviously, some dances succeed and others do not.

10. Calvin Tompkins, *The Bride and the Bachelors* (New York: Viking, 1965), p. 124.

11. Margaret Henle, "Birth and Death of Ideas," in *Contemporary Approaches to Creative Thinking*, ed. Howard E. Gruber, Glenn Terrell, and Michael Wertheimer (New York: Atherton, 1962), p. 38.

Choreographing as a free agent means extracting from our experiences the appropriate creative responses without imposing intellectually predetermined concepts. We must liberate ourselves from all dependence on the familiar. We must be actively willing to understand and credit the new and the revolutionary.

Although blind acceptance is certainly unwise, it is equally as pointless to remain unaware of a cultural development until fifty years after the fact. This cultural insularity is a major deterrent to the development of quality dance education. The lag must be overcome because it is impossible to fully grasp innovations long after their introduction, for unlike music and art, dance is transitory and ephemeral, and leaves no concrete product for future study and enjoyment.

Some Pioneers in Nonliteral Dance

Beginning in the early 1950s, the pioneers in nonliteral dance included Alwin Nikolais, Merce Cunningham, and Sybil Shearer; they were followed by Erick Hawkins, Murray Louis, and Paul Taylor.

Alwin Nikolais

Fortified with a sound dance foundation from the Hanya Holm school and having had considerable choreographic experience, Nikolais began to develop his own unique form of dance theater after World War II. Not only did he experiment with movement, but also with other elements of theater—sound, light, costume, stage set, and devices for extending movement beyond the body. He began his new trend of experimentation shortly after his arrival at the Henry Street Playhouse in 1948; since that time he has developed a very productive dance school, an outstanding dance company of his own, a playhouse company, and an enthusiastic dance audience that usually numbers at least as many men as women.

Nikolais's form of dance theater is highly stylized and individual; one immediately recognizes a Nikolais work. His choreography is motionally and spatially articulate; it reflects the choreographer's kinetic sensitivity, his dynamic imagination for movement and motion, and his keen sensitivity to design, color, and sound. While he is a movement and motion purist in his teaching and in the development of dancers, he chooses to fulfill all of his talents in his own choreography. He does just that in giving all elements of theater an integral and dynamic part in his dance theater productions.

Necessity played a basic role in the creation of the Nikolais dance theater. In the early fifties the exercise of his many talents for choreography, stage and costume design, and musical scores, was more a case of need than choice, since money for such collaboration was unavailable to choreographers at that time. It was through his handling of all parts of dance productions that Nikolais gained first-hand knowledge and practical experience in using all elements of theater. Certainly these experiences helped to shape his conception and development of the dance theater he produces today.

To experience a Nikolais concert is to be swept up by a magic carpet and transported into the middle of a new and wonderful world—a world in which bodies are transcended into motion-producing optical illusions; a world of changing motional values into colorful splendor, beautiful designs, magnificent sculptural shapes; a world of fleeting images, surprises, human subtleties, unusual sounds, fleet-footed jointlessness, sylph-like gyrations, sentient images, dynamic excitement, mixtures of action, light, color, and sound into a glorious collage, and the feeling that you are on the inside of the whole experience.

Nikolais's dance theater is the epitome of nonliteralness. It is free from domination of the concrete and traditional vehicles of communication. He allows the materials of dance to speak in their own terms—in movement and motion. He does not settle for the limitations of the human body nor its human condition. Rather, he works to enlarge the dancer's orientation to the universe as well as to establish that particular dance world in the contemporary period of the mid-twentieth century; his work rests on the premise that "the province of art is to explore the inner mechanisms and extra dimensional areas of life, and out of the exploration, to produce its findings translated into the form of the artist's medium."[12]

His early innovations were met with critical reviews that reflected a lack of readiness to understand his departure from the literal cycle of modern dance. At the same time, the freshness of experimental ideas was sensed as necessary and vital. Once the initial shock had subsided, dance reviewers became more receptive, and modern dance was launched into its new cycle of nonliteral development. (Alwin Nikolais and Murray Louis have recently joined forces in establishing the Louis-Nikolais Dance Theater Lab consisting of a professional school as well as their own performing companies in midtown Manhattan.)

John Martin, then dance critic of the *New York Times*, paid Nikolais the highest compliment by crediting him with fresh and original talent and an awareness of the true substance of dance. He described Nikolais's work as being "the discovery of what we call, with great exactness, the modern dance in terms of its own theatre."[13]

Merce Cunningham

Merce Cunningham, with his extensive experimental range, has successfully pursued the extreme and the unusual. His experimentation with dance by chance in the early 1950s represented a radical break from the typical modern dance of the day because it deliberately aimed at minimizing the influence of the choreographer at a time when, most typically, the goal was to make that influence centrally important. He called his experiment *Suite by Chance* (1953). It was a formal dance, classic in character and choreog-

---

12. Murray Louis, "The Contemporary Dance Theatre of Alwin Nikolais," *Dance Observer* 27, no. 1 (Jan. 1960): 5–6.

13. John Martin, *New York Times*, Jan. 6, 1957, II, 14:5.

raphed for four dancers. *Suite by Chance* was experimental in that it used a chance method of composition; movement and count determinations were made by coin-tossing. It was danced to an original score for electronic sound composed by Christian Wolff. Chance procedures had also been used by Cunningham in previous dances including *Collage I* and *Collage II* and in the fourteenth dance of *16 Dances for Soloist and Company of Three. Suite by Chance* became a study of interrelationships of movement, time, and space. This beginning led to many other experiments.

Cunningham has been the recipient of two Guggenheim fellowships. The first made possible continued study of the use of timing concepts free of metric pulse, as well as the use of chance for continuity.

Today Cunningham's choreography is unpredictable. Those who knew him before he formed his own dance company realize how radical a departure he has made from his former training in ballet and his association with the Martha Graham company.

Cunningham's dance world is one of unending imagination, change, unconventional subject matter, and conspicuous absence of emotional display. Sometimes form evolves (it is never imposed) and dynamic development occurs, and sometimes it does not. There is no specific patterning to his recent dances. In spite of this, one is left with experiences embodying emotional impact, movement design of a novel kind, and fleeting imagery. Sometimes his choreography is striking, sometimes provoking or even beautiful; at other times it is difficult to grasp. His gift for subtle comedy and his adventuresome imagination are always a delight.

Cunningham does not use literal materials such as stories or psychological problems.

Dancing has a continuity of its own that need not be dependent upon either the rise and fall of sound (music) or the pitch and cry of words (literary ideas). Its force of feeling lies in the physical image, fleeting or static. It can and does evoke all sorts of individual responses in the single spectator. These dances may be seen in this light.

The music and the dance co-exist as individual but interpenetrating happenings, jointly experienced in the length of time they take up and divide.[14]

For Cunningham the subject of dance is dancing, and he does it quite casually. The dancers dance, things happen, images form, and structures unfold in a time-space context that is fulfilled by each dancer. One can never anticipate what will happen next and is thus rendered defenseless. The spectator makes associations with the many images that occur and lets them grow and develop into a gestalt of understanding. His performances are marked by intensity of concentration, a wonderful sense of abandon, and an unusual but fascinating mix of movement events. He, too, moves out of the concrete world, away from human problems, and into a larger world of which we all are a part. He stresses movement and an independent relationship between music and dance; however, dance must carry the weight of communication. Unconcerned with changing the world, he simply presents a movement statement that affirms what is, thus increasing one's awareness of life and the world in which he lives.

Cunningham has met with considerable enthusiasm on his many international tours and is very highly esteemed in France. Indeed, his work was appreciated in foreign countries before he was duly credited in the United States. A highly independent, as well as individual, artist, he continues to dance, choreograph, and experiment freely as he chooses, paying little attention to critical reaction.

Sybil Shearer

To witness Sybil Shearer's dancing is like taking a quick trip into space—it is an illusory, exciting, and dynamic experience. Her movement, which unfolds precisely and with carefully controlled intensity, is highly individual in its timing values and dynamic

14. Merce Cunningham, Concert Program Notes, Douglass College, April 8, 1965.

action. Its detailed phrasing uses unorthodox rhythms. Motion dominates, making her performance fluid, metakinetic, elusive, and very difficult to remember. One is left fully satisfied with the experience itself with little desire to leave the dance world and return to reality.

There is no patterning of dances, nor is there any one style that runs consistently throughout her works. Each new creation is exactly that, and seldom is like any other. Miss Shearer is careful to avoid following a system. She does not categorize movement or its forms of communication. Her well of experience is simply there, and her creation of new dances emerges freely without resemblance to anything else she has done. She is neither brainwashed by training and background experiences nor a slave to personal habits.

Miss Shearer's choreography is always conceived abstractly; the content appears to have been dug out of the depths of her subconscious and translated directly and intuitively into movement. Her movement theme becomes the creative nucleus of the work, and she explores it exhaustively. Each theme, evolving gradually, is clear, precisely timed, and communicated with the honesty and directness characteristic of the innocent child.

In her constant pursuit of perfection Miss Shearer has developed her body into a finely tuned, exquisitely controlled instrument that responds instantly to internal motivation. Her magnificent carriage and balance contribute to the illusion that gravity does not wholeheartedly exist, and she can toss off staggeringly complicated movement sequences with ease. Her ability to articulate movement is so highly developed that dynamic motion becomes the main vehicle of communication.

Miss Shearer's work is properly classified as contemporary, although the beauty of line and lyricism she achieves has a classical feeling. An unusually strong sense of design is the only resemblance to her early training with the former Humphrey-Weidman company. In this characteristic she does not rely on the pictorial aspect of design alone; to Miss Shearer, design is a refined sense of proportion, time, space, and direction. She creates sculpturally integrative design that becomes dynamically alive with movement and motion; the effect is exciting both visually and kinetically.

Spontaneity underlies all of Miss Shearer's work. She creates most of her dance phrases by improvising. Through many years of practice she has become highly skilled in the art of improvisation. It has become the key to creating the "right" movements and the means for carefully fostering the development of spontaneity to such a degree of perfection that it appears to be a controlled choreographic element. The improvised movement she creates is immediately complex, detailed, and possessed of the element of surprise.

Miss Shearer's choreography is emotionally detached—yet one experiences strong underlying feelings. Her dances neither moralize nor tell stories. They communicate directly through the senses; they are perceived experiences. Her titles are often poetic, philosophical, sometimes metaphorical and seemingly literal on the surface (*In Place of Opinions, Return of the Herd*), but her treatment of dance content is definitely nonliteral. Her style is distinctive because it is so directly the result of her individuality and she is distinctly individual. It is compounded of strong design, dynamic motion, and skillful use of music. Her profound understanding and feeling for music and the musical phrase enable her to make musical accompaniment the perfect complement to her choreography—she neither fights the accompaniment nor surrenders to it. Supportive of her artistic individuality is her freedom to create as she wishes without regard for box office demands, critical opinion, causes, or popularity. Her art can thrive regardless of what anyone thinks of it.

As artist-in-residence at the National College of Education in Evanston, Illinois, Miss Shearer enjoys the use of the college's eight-hundred-seat theater. The theater's stage was redesigned to meet her specific requests for unique curtain and lighting arrangements and a performing area equal to Lincoln Center's New York State Theater. Here she enjoys the satisfactions of working with a dedicated and talented young company.

In the twenty-two years that she has lived and danced in Illinois, Sybil Shearer, with the help of her stage and lighting designer, Helen Morrison, has fostered an enthusiastic and constantly growing dance audience in the midwest—a pioneer achievement.

Erick Hawkins

Erick Hawkins's dance today is totally different from his earlier work during his years as a leading dancer with the Martha Graham company; his beginning efforts were simply dismissed by many reviewers as little more than pretentious.

Hawkins neither expresses feeling overtly, nor does he use much motion in most of his choreography. He achieves dynamism in a quiet sort of way. He creates an atmosphere out of poetically presented images that spark the spectator's imagination and provoke his feelings. As a master of dynamic stillness, he uses his beautifully articulate physique to perform movement that is strongly designed and mystical in quality. His accompaniment is as individual as his dancing; it is created for him by Lucia Dlugoszewski, who uses any instrument that yields the sound she is after, and who is as interesting to watch as to hear.

As late as the early 1960s, dance critics had real difficulty understanding Hawkins's work. Reviews of his concerts were little more than a series of unanswered questions. In an article in *Dance Observer*, Hawkins helped to shed light on his point of view and clear the way for fuller appreciation of his work.[15]

That article articulated a point of view which is basically existential and supportive to the concept of immediacy. Hawkins considers dance as the truth within each person's body that will never happen again. Dance exists only in the "now" and no place else— therefore, "the momentness of dance is one of its most precious gifts. Actually, only the nowness of ourselves exists, but true-seeing

15. Erick Hawkins, "A Little House to Understand and Protect It," *Dance Observer* 27, no. 2 (Feb. 1960): 21.

of time, is the inside of our seeing."[16] It is this inside-seeing which is the act of his performance. He would "build a little house that is understandable out of the material lying around in the streets of culture—the written words."[17]

For Hawkins, dance happens now—on stage, instant by instant, if it happens at all. The unique dimension and material of dance are gravity and the body and mind that live it. It is concrete, subjective, and, therefore, pure fact. "The dance of pure fact is dance before it is language, before it has meanings."[18] There is nothing to communicate, no symbols. Movement is not the subject matter; movement simply is. One does not dominate gravity but rather cooperates with it. One has the paradox of power through delicacy and simplicity. By letting every part of the body exist for its own sake, every part of the body is brought to the threshold of awareness. This is the immediately apprehended—the pure fact.[19]

Immediacy, which holds a strong position in Hawkins's philosophy of dance, means the complete presence and awareness of mind and body in moment-to-moment relationship, simultaneously here, now; "the mind must be empty enough to let the body inhabit it—the moving body—that envelope of space, time, and gravity."[20] "The motionlessness (result of resolved paradox of thought and action) on stage is often the most haunting point of a moment to moment existence—the real floating life."[21]

Murray Louis

Murray Louis is equally gifted both as dancer and as choreographer. Among his array of assets is a phenomenal body that is

16. Ibid.
17. Ibid.
18. Erick Hawkins, "Pure Fact," *Dance Observer* 25, no. 9 (Nov. 1958): 133–34.
19. Ibid., p. 134.
20. Ibid.
21. Ibid.

Alwin Nikolais.

From Nikolais's *Somniloquy*.

From Nikolais's *Tent*.

From Murray Louis's *Proximities*.

From Murray Louis's *Calligraph for Martyrs*.

(Sosenko)

Erick Hawkins in "pine tree" from *8 Clear Places*.

From Erick Hawkins's *Geography of Noon*.

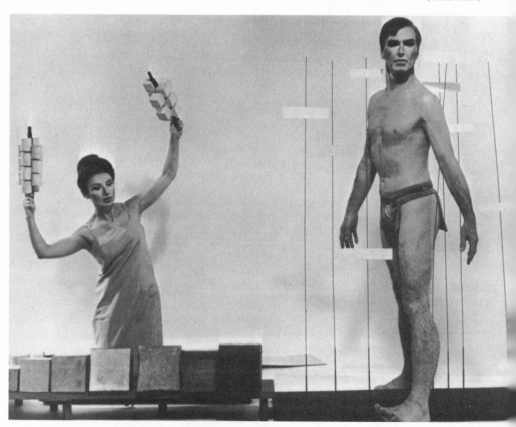

From Sybil Shearer's *Fables and Proverbs*.

From Sybil Shearer's *Return of the Herd.*

Sybil Shearer at her studio home, Northbrook, Illinois.

Don Redlich and Gladys Bailin in *Couplet*.

Don Redlich in *Earthling.*

From Merce Cunningham's *Place*.

From Merce Cunningham's *Collage III*.

Paul Taylor.

From Paul Taylor's *Orbs*.

flexible but strong and electrically alive in every muscle fiber. His disciplined and controlled body frees him to respond to the dictates of an imagination that ranges from highly creative to very wild. And his movement style is so lyrical and musically articulated that his body appears to sing its movements; he is a master of spontaneity.

Louis can create in a variety of choreographic forms, which he explores freely; the resultant choreography may range from somewhat literal to extremely nonliteral. His outstanding works lean toward the nonliteral. *Landscapes* is a beautiful mood piece, exactly designed and articulated with quickly changing motion; *Proximities* is a lyrical work of people and place relationships in which the movement is typically a Murray Louis invention set to the music of Brahms. The combination of the traditional music and contemporary character of the dance itself makes a beautiful kind of lyric dance theater with a classical flavor. The clashing of two worlds is beautifully communicated in *Intersection*; it raises all kinds of emotional responses and questions. In this dance Louis manages to build the experience in the spectator in a very unemotional way; he communicates the absurdness of time gap, cultural gap, and the incredibility of diverse but simultaneous types of existence. All of this grows steadily at a very slow pace becoming eclipsed in reverse at the end all within a minute. Mr. Louis demonstrates his ability to develop great depth in treatment of his content.

As one watches Murray Louis dance, one is aware of his quality of fluid motion, lightness, rebound, electric-like movement impulses and his ability to stretch a movement beyond the expected limit, to make many simultaneous but interconnected motions, to use the head and hands as an anecdote to the phrase. He can create wild characters in the abstract and perform them with great impact; his strong personality with his underlying pure brand of Louis humor invariably shines through his works. And though he has been artistically nurtured under Nikolais's tutelage, he has his own distinctive style, as well as his own ideas about choreography. Through his innate sense of the underlying drama of feelings and his simultaneous motor conception of them, he produces a vibrant, intricate, and complex form of movement that communicates directly.

Murray Louis's personality combines dynamic directness, spontaneity, and hilarious humor. He is as spontaneous and direct in his teaching as he is in his dancing, and his teaching experience is extensive. He has performed internationally and on television both as the leading dancer with the Nikolais company and also with his own company.

Thoroughly unpredictable and delightfully original, Murray Louis uses his remarkably articulated body to experiment freely, daringly, and wittily in movement. "He is never guilty of a message; he simply registers, records, and transmits data, along with his highly individual deductions and opinions."[22]

Paul Taylor

Paul Taylor made his initial dynamic impression doing choreography of an abstract or nonliteral nature in the late 1950s. However, some significant works which are still performed were on the scene in the early 1950s. The dynamic impression resulted more from Taylor's dancing ability than from his choreography. Just when he was beginning to be considered avant-garde, his choreography shifted to a different style—more romantic and sometimes even classical. Obviously, the key to Paul Taylor does not rest in his choreographic style per se.

Recently, Taylor wrote a chapter appropriately entitled "Down with Choreography."[23] He believes some dances look like "choreography" because the dancers are shaped and formed into a preconceived role that has little to do with them individually. "I like

22. Quoted from John Martin in *Murray Louis* (theater booklet of the Henry Street Playhouse, 1965).

23. Paul Taylor, "Down with Choreography," in Selma J. Cohen, *The Modern Dance: Seven Statements of Belief* (Middletown, Conn.: Wesleyan University Press, 1966), p. 91.

to think of a dance as a vehicle, not necessarily for one star, but for everybody. You try to find aspects in individual dancers that can be exploited."[24] According to this point of view, he starts with an assessment of his dancers' values; he then designs his dances as vehicles for the best use of these assets, and he works intuitively, permitting his choreography to evolve and take shape.

While most of Taylor's choreography tends to be of a nonliteral nature, he does not work in the nonliteral area exclusively. Some of his work is highly literal, and some dramatic. But whether literal or nonliteral, his choreography communicates effectively as sculptural design, and in terms of kinetics, feeling, and form. And though his dances provoke strong feelings, they are basically unemotional in themselves.

I would like to make it clear from the start that these dances are primarily meant to be a kind of food for the eye. If they evoke dramatic images and riddles, the key to their solution lies not so much in the brain, but in the senses and the eye of the spectator. It was not my intention to present literary messages, although certain dances here have as their focal point a common subject with certain writings.[25]

Taylor's concerts are experiences in variety. Occasionally one feels the presence of the Graham influence both in choreographic approach as well as in his dancing (*Junction* 1962). But Taylor's whole approach incorporates a great deal of lyrical freedom characteristically his own. One of his earlier works (*Epitaphs* 1956) is highly representative of Taylor's individuality. In this work he ingeniously has extracted the real essence of remnants of the past and tastefully put them into organic movement form that is subtly understated. The costume which completely covers the body and face depersonalizes the dancers and frees the movement to communicate completely; his particular choice of just the right movement in combination with sparsely used folk music is an almost

24. Ibid., p. 97.
25. Paul Taylor, publicity materials (Charles Reinhart Management, Inc., New York, 1967).

perfect mix. *Epitaphs* is a timeless dance that is as fresh today as it was in 1956.

Taylor uses whatever seems appropriate to his purpose. He uses traditional and classical music as well as contemporary and electronic scores. His most recent work (*Foreign Exchange*, 1970) is done to electronic music. It is a contemporary work using a stage set that suggests gray stone, having the air of the stone age and the primitive sense of discovery of self, others, groups, community. It is a series of interesting dances exploring relationships in a subtle and abstract form. The interwoven chain at the end of the first section is a particularly pleasing surprise. The work is unemotional, cool but not cold.

Taylor himself is strong yet fluidly controlled. His body is capable of extraordinary, dynamic movement. He has an innate sense of comedy as strongly illustrated in *Three Epitaphs*. Although his humor is understated and subtle, he uses it inventively and often daringly.

Taylor's company is a group of well-trained strong dancers. His movement is full of energy, muscularly demanding, yet possessing considerable freedom. There is no emoting, yet one experiences feeling. He has a rather tender approach to movement relationships, and his dancers produce his works sensitively. Taylor has been highly successful in touring with his company both in the United States and abroad.

Characteristic of all of these modern dance artists of the contemporary period is their stubborn independence, their staunch refusal to become mere replicas of the masters of the first cycle of modern dance. They are neither disciples of their training, nor are they interested in producing disciples; they are developing and producing original performing artists. Among these outstanding young dance artists who have reached prominence today are: Gladys Bailin and Phyllis Lamhut of the Nikolais and Louis companies; Carolyn Carlson of the Nikolais company; Carolyn Brown and

Viola Farber of the Cunningham company; Nancy Meehan, Kelly Holt, and James Tyler of the Hawkins company; Betty De Jong and Dan Waggoner of the Taylor company; Toby Nicholson and Masao of the Shearer company; Don Redlich, from the Hanya Holm school of dance, an independent dancer who has started a new company with Gladys Bailin; and Joy Boutilier and Mimi Garrard, both with their own companies and both deriving from the Henry Street Playhouse School of Dance.

The Experimentalists

Any advancing field of art has on the periphery people with differing points of view, the antiestablishment group who are busily engaged in testing tradition and developing their own forms of expression. Today's group of experimentalists found their incubation center at the Judson Church in New York City beginning in 1962 and phasing out about 1967. Those getting their start through the Judson who are still on the scene performing are: Yvonne Rainer, Robert and Judith Dunn, James Waring, Steve Paxton, Deborah Hay, Aileen Pasloff, and Meredith Monk. In addition, Twyla Tharp, a later arrival, emerged from an eclectic background, but with strong influence from Paul Taylor and also considerable individuality. Ann Halprin of San Francisco, a modern dancer in the first cycle, has moved into experimentation with a kind of hybrid dance-drama-happening. Even though Halprin and Tharp did not derive from the Judson and do have dance training, they are included here because they are currently experimenting along highly individual lines of pursuit.

In most cases these individuals are not only antitraditional but they also reject many of the highly experimental bases on which the contemporary modern dance artists of today operate. The experimental movement is characterized by diverse approaches to dance that stem from direct opposition to previously accepted principles; the products in many cases are considered nondance, even by those doing it. Some characteristics of these approaches include:

1) the rejection of technique as essential for a dancer, 2) the belief that art and life are one and the same, 3) the ordering of movements or events by putting together a series of unrelated tasks on a time plan, 4) the use of many forms of activity simultaneously, 5) playacting, 6) dissolving the distance between audience and performer, 7) the rejection of content and form as necessary structures, 8) making things for the moment with no thought of permanence, 9) no requirement of a beginning or end in dances. The experimental movement is a rebellion against most traditional and some contemporary principles; it seems to be existing for the purpose of testing art values.

These experimentalists were strongly influenced by the ideas of John Cage, to some extent by Merce Cunningham, and by the trends toward change taking place in the various other forms of art. Central to Cage's point of view is that of eliminating the subjective influence of the artist on his art. This point of view has led to chance choreography and the concept of indeterminacy in music and its relationship to the dance. These experiments have produced some strange products; some are strongly related to happenings, some to theater, but most are only distantly related to what is still perceived by most people as dance. This situation, in addition to the use of multi-media, a natural development of our time, has given rise to the question of when dance is dance and when it is not. This can be a very disturbing problem since some experimentalists are doing work that can be considered dance in its generally accepted sense, and others are not; yet they call themselves dancers and get bookings as dance companies. In small towns and cities, where people only know the dance of twenty-five years ago, booking such a company could be a tragic experience for the spectator, the dancers, and the field of modern dance. An audience needs to be prepared for the type of thing it will see.

The dilemma of what to call these new experiments remains. Yvonne Rainer has solved her problem by calling her program a mixed-media group performance; this appears to be a more accurate label than dance. While none of this experimental group has achieved any great acclaim, the fact remains that experiments testing traditional beliefs have led to new forms of movement expression. Some include dance as a small part of the whole; some simply change the definition of dance to include what they wish; some are interesting as well as different in the way communication is achieved. How much influence these explorations will have on the future of dance is as yet unknown.

The Nonliteral Process

Unlike literal dance, nonliteral dance is neither pantomimic nor descriptive, and carries no specific message that can be communicated verbally. In producing a nonliteral dance one does not start with literal movement and create variations upon it; rather, the entire dance is conceived in a nonliteral form. Although the inspirational source is most often nonliteral, it can be quite literal, the nonliteral character of the dance resulting from what one selects from the literal source and how one develops it. It is not the source, then, but the conception and treatment of materials that determines whether or not a dance is nonliteral.

This form of treatment requires an ordering of movement through a neuromuscular sense of logic. The human body, as the instrument of communication, has to transcend its traditional personal limitations; it must be trained, therefore, to make neuromuscular discriminations; to sense degrees of action, textures, qualities; and to become kinetically alive and kinesthetically aware. Besides developing strength, control, flexibility, and agility, the dancer's body must be disciplined to experience in many ways and in many contexts the complete range of possible complex motion. It must respond sensitively to the dancer's feelings and needs and to the demands of the choreographer.

What the dancer must aim for are clearly stated movements stripped of idiosyncrasies and superfluous motion, directly projected and spatially oriented movement that is organically related to the dance content. Articulation of movement must be so subtle and refined that the viewer is virtually unaware of movement transitions as such. Movement should unfold, emerge, or occur without apparent physical effort. In this intensive exploration of movement qualities and relationships, the choreographer should not overlook the importance of silence and of pauses or holds in movement as significant dance materials.

Motivation in dance is reflected through phrasing—the grouping of movement according to motor logic. Because phrases may be of any length in nonliteral dance, movement is freed from the confines of metric demands and musical phrasing. In other words, nonliteral dance is conceived neuromuscularly and guided by kinetic intuition.

Motion (action in a dynamic time-space complex) is the principal vehicle of communication in the purist forms of nonliteral dance. Embodying form, quality, shape, and motivation, it lends continuity to choreography and is considered of great importance. It is explored in terms of line, direction, focus, quality, shape, texture, and rhythm.

The primary goals of kinetic sensitivity to time values and to their fulfillment in motion require considerable time and effort to develop. Timing is individual to each choreographer; it must be sensed by the dancer as patterns of energy release which must be executed within a framework of time limits. The possible varieties of energy release patterns within a given time structure are enormous. Meter may be mixed; phrases may vary considerably in length; accent and rhythm can be manipulated almost endlessly.

Space is of primary concern because dancers are related to each other through spatial design as well as through movement and motion. Movement is addressed directly to space, unfolding into a specific unified spatial pattern. The interaction of such spatial elements as projection, intensity, direction, and shape can be altered by the use of lighting; changes in lighting, the size of auditorium and stage, interaction between dancers and audience and between sound and motion, and the color balance in costumes and draperies are some of the variable factors that produce changes in dimension, distortion of figures, and the creation of visual illusions.

The Nonliteral Product

The nonliteral dance product is an organic unit that must be experienced as a whole. The total sensory import is strongly affected by light, color, and sound. Intellectualization by the observer, if it takes place at all, should take place only after the sensory experience.

The content of nonliteral dance need not be profound; depth of treatment and development of content are far more important than the content itself. The inspirational source can be literal or it can be nonliteral, nonspecific, stemming from the dancer's subconscious. Content is limited, then, by the individual choreographer's ability to deal with the more intangible subjects.

The materials of nonliteral dance choreography include images (visual, motor, auditory, intellectual), feelings (emotional and physical), movement shape, structural form, body relationships, design, space, and time. These materials and their virtually endless variations comprise the vocabulary of the dancer and the choreographer. The choreographer works intuitively while carefully selecting materials which make movement sense.

The dance form that results from this intuitive process most often evolves and develops rather than follows a preconceived pattern or plan. Although there are no prescribed restrictions or requirements placed on form, musical or prescribed forms can be used if the choreographer prefers or needs to use them.

What about the use of titles in nonliteral dance? Dances are untitled so that the spectator can view the dance without bias or preconceptions. Actually, this form of dance does not need titles any more than a concerto or symphony needs them. It makes better sense to leave dances untitled or to use an umbrella title incorporating several dances so that the spectator is free to do his own relating and associating.

When titles are used, they rarely denote meaning or subject; more often they are used metaphorically or as a means of identifying the general area of experience being considered. They are used as a compromise to help the spectator move into the nonliteral realm by providing a starting place, a point of reference. And they are often based on symbolism, imagery, motion, quality, feeling, or form of a dance as well as idea; literal titles defeat the choreographer's purpose by forcing the spectator to read specific meaning into his work.

The nonliteral dance product, then, is characterized by 1) subscription to choreographic principles that are more liberal than those underlying traditional forms of modern dance, 2) freedom of the choreographer to implement his ideas according to his own conception and artistic principles, 3) kinetic development from a movement source as opposed to intellectually planned choreography, 4) absence of emotional, dramatic gestures that have specific meanings, 5) multidimensional, dynamic motion, complex coordination, and direct communication, 6) choreographic unity—the whole disciplined to its content, 7) sensory experience—a matrix of color, shape, sound, motion, rhythm, style, design, feeling, and 8) artistic form in which motion contains a unique quality of feeling.

2

Materials and Structure
of Nonliteral Dance

Basic Materials

The dancer's basic equipment is the body as his instrument and
the physical principles of movement as his tools. Included in these
mechanical laws of movement are gravity, equilibrium, motion,
leverage, force, angle of rebound, and spin.[1]

The body, or instrument, is endowed with capacities to think,
sense, balance, coordinate, and time. The first task of the dancer
is to become aware of the tremendous expressive potential of his
body and to develop his physical capabilities to their maximum;
this heightened awareness will result in greater freedom both in
invention and performance. He must learn to use his body as a well-
tuned instrument of communication without confining it to the
human condition. To do this he must accept design for its own sake
rather than as a mere adornment of his body.

Among the body skills to be developed are those of kinesthetically
finding the body's center, aligning body segments, lengthening the
spine, relating the body as a totality to its surrounding space, and
interacting with that space. The body must become highly sensitive
to dimensions of height, depth, and width and the elements of
movement and motion such as volume, shape, line, quality, texture,
timing, and spatial design; all must be sensed kinesthetically by
the body.

1. Marian R. Broer, *Efficiency of Human Movement*, 2d ed. (Philadelphia:
W. B. Saunders, 1966), pp. 35–94.

The result of this rigorous training of the body as a communicative instrument stripped of human mannerisms is the depersonalization that typifies nonliteral dance. Freed from the need to express personality, the dancer is released from the confinement of intellectual ordering of movement and from the limitations imposed in conveying emotions. The choreographer is free to explore movement and motion for their inherent values or to satisfy his own creative whims. This rejection of the literal which has typified the second cycle of modern dance resembles the liberating trends that have emancipated music and the visual arts in recent decades. The new freedom requires dramatic changes in choreographic principles, use of materials, and the training of dancers.

Structure of Dance

For purposes of analysis, the structure of a dance may be classified into its physical and psychological components.

Physical components include:

1. *Movements basic to the natural body structure,* namely,

a. *axial movement* (bend, stretch, twist, turn, rise, fall, swing, sway, circumduct)

b. *locomotor movement* (walk, run, leap, hop, jump)

c. movement qualities (swinging, sustained, percussive, vibratory, collapsing).

2. Types of action derived from 1a, b, and c—such as arch, bounce, brush, chug, curl, drag, elevate, emerge, explode, fall, gallop, hang, lean, lunge, press, pull, pulsate, push, reach, rebound, rock, roll, shift, shrink, skip, slide, spin, tilt, twirl, tumble, undulate, vibrate.

3. *Qualities, shapes, and textures of movement and motion.* The activities above can be performed in the following qualities, shapes, or textures: angular, billowy, brittle, bulbous, curved, dense, elastic, fat, flat, flimsy, hard, heavy, jagged, jerky, light, linear, lofty, rigid,

round, shaky, smooth, soft, still, straight, strong, successive, sustained, tense, thick, thin, weak, wispy.

4. *Choreographic factors that shape movement and motion*:

a. *Articulation*—the coordination of movements with regard to their appropriate motional values.

b. *Design*—interrelationship between individual positions and overall movement or between bodies in their relative time-space context.

c. *Dimension*—movement along an axis of height, depth or width.

d. *Direction*—the line of action in space such as forward, backward, sideward, diagonally forward, diagonally backward, upward, downward, and circular.

e. *Dynamics*—the interaction of forces of movement and motion that produce contrast.

f. *Focus*—intensity and direction of movement as it is projected spatially.

g. *Level*—the plane in which movement occurs in relation to elevation; this may vary from low to high within the possible range of human elevation.

h. *Space*—the character of the area defined or created by a given movement's symmetry or asymmetry, line, balance, quality, shape, volume.

i. *Time*—the relative duration of movements and their distinctive rhythm, accent, meter, or nonmeter, and pauses.

Psychological components include:

1. *Mental activities* that influence movement and motion, such as aesthetic judgment, associations, attitudes, awareness, central coordination of all functions, conception of work, creativity, discipline of body to perform as willed, evaluation, inventiveness, memory, motivation, problem-solving, relating of materials, and selection.

2. *Emotional states* such as amorous, angry, apprehensive, benevolent, bashful, bored, carefree, compulsive, conniving, contented,

depressed, desirous, desperate, empty, engrossed, flippant, flirta-
tious, forlorn, frightened, frustated, gloomy, grandiose, hateful,
humble, independent, inferior, insecure, irresponsible, joyous, lone-
ly, loving, loyal, majestic, morose, obsessed, pensive, protective,
proud, puzzled, rejected, sedate, sensuous, silly, worried.

The materials of dance identified above may be used in various
ways to help the student experience meaning in dance as well as to
understand their uses in choreography.

3

Approaches to Choreography

Nonliteral Choreography

What distinguishes nonliteral choreography from the traditional forms of modern dance? First of all, nonliteral choreography has a much broader range of subjects and sources than its literal counterpart. A second difference lies in the special treatment of theatrical devices such as unusual costumes, props, lighting, and special effects. Unlike the representational choreographers, the nonliteral artist does not use these devices as a substitute for movement or as conveyers of meaning in themselves. The objects and materials are used rather as extensions of movement and motion. Since the nonliteral choreographer seeks direct communication rather than translation of meaning through objects representing something else, any symbolic meaning would be unintentional.

The contemporary choreographer assumes that dance may exist for its own sake and needs no other motive or justification. Free to develop his content intuitively and unencumbered by considerations of literal reality and intellectual logic, he produces a dance that communicates directly to the senses, that relates no specific message or story, and that presents no dramatic sequence of events. The dancer's body, deemphasized as a human form, is important only for its ability to produce well-articulated movement and motion; it becomes an instrument of communication, not limited to portrayal of people, personalities, and emotional states. The resultant freedom of this point of view enables the dancer to transcend his physical limits in exploring a whole new realm of communication.

A Word About Choreographic Procedure

The information presented in this chapter is intended to provide new avenues for the exploration and discovery of movement that is useful in the creation of nonliteral dance. Emphasis is placed on experiencing movement and motion in their many complex forms, building associations with the basic materials of the movement medium, and avoiding materials that might deflect dance along literal paths.

Improvisation is presented first because, in its elimination of intellectual planning, it provides an immediate route to the spontaneous movement characteristic of nonliteral dance. The time spent in developing improvisational skill affords the extensive movement and feeling experiences that will be useful later in solving dance problems.

Dance problems presented in this chapter are intended to familiarize the student with the concepts and ideas, and with the invention and development of movement themes that are basic to choreographing larger dances. The problems, serving as short but condensed dance study experiences, are designed to overcome the many different kinds of choreographic and technical pitfalls that face the student and, at the same time, save a great deal of time and energy that might be consumed by working with longer dances.

The technical problems that conclude this chapter are exercises in the application of principles that lead to skilled performance. Their major purpose is to develop neuromuscular sensitivity to movement and motion and to discipline the body in the act of performing.

Improvisation

Besides developing the essential spontaneity, improvisation provides rich and varied movement experiences without the need for the time-consuming process of designing and polishing movements required by choreography. It offers extensive practice in creating and discarding dance phrases, in conceiving dance phrases neuro-muscularly, and in responding to the movement of other dancers. As a means of creative exploration—a road to movement discovery and variation—improvisation can often be as valuable when it is observed as when it is experienced firsthand.

Dance improvisation is a complex process of responding to a specific stimulus. Since the stimulus cannot remain pure (it is almost immediately transformed by past knowledge and experiences and feelings), the individual's response to it is necessarily complex—charged with feelings and associations that are largely subconscious. The same stimulus is therefore unlikely to yield the same or even simliar responses in different people. And it might not even yield the same response in the same individual receiving it several times under differing circumstances.

As a beginning, improvisation might be explored through some of the sources listed below. Although these sources may be quite literal, one's conception and treatment of them must be nonliteral.

Chance happenings	Movement design
Dramatic situations	Movement kinetics
Emotional qualities	Movement styles
Human relationships	Spatial and structural forms
Ideas	Symbols
Illusions	Timing and rhythmic factors
Images	Combinations of any of the above
Material objects	

In improvising, one might start with one stimulus and add others during his process of association. In this way movement sequences that could develop as content for a dance are built. The following categories of stimuli are suggested simply as starters.

Auditory Stimuli

Music: from various periods and styles ranging from polyphonic to contemporary; lyrical, ethnic, descriptive, electronic, percussive, and so on.

Words: Words may be explored for their meaning, sound, symbolic significance, or poetic value.

Poetry: Poems may be responded to in terms of meter, mood or feeling, interpretation, imagery, or total impression.

Sounds: The variety of sounds is endless in this electronic age. New sounds can be created and recorded, distorted, and manipulated. There are as well sounds of nature, sounds of activity (such as breaking glass, alarm clocks, telephones, the rattle of money, sirens, dogs barking, hissing radiators), the sound of machines and instruments. Many of these sounds are available on recordings. One must be sure that he is responding to the sound itself, rather than to what the sound represents since the concern in nonliteral dance is with the purity of sound, not its meaning.

Tactile Stimuli

To get a true response one must actually feel the object rather than rely on memory of the object's texture. It is generally better to close the eyes in order to eliminate distractions. Some of the following objects might be useful as tactile stimuli:

Brush	Rope
Burlap	Rubber bands
Crumpled newspaper	Sculpture
Foam	Silk
Fur	Snow
Marble	Sponge
Mohair yarn	Velvet
Pine needles	Wire

Visual Stimuli

Any object used for tactile stimulation may also be used as a visual stimulus. Those items marked with asterisks are particularly appropriate for use as an object in the improvisation itself.

Architecture	Bucket	*Eyeglasses
Blackboard	Design	*Flag

*Flowers	Paintings	*Suitcase
*Furniture	Photographs	*Swedish box
*Gown	*Pole	Table
Magazine	*Rope	Typewriter
Newspaper	*Sculpture	

Emotional States

One must rely on memory of emotional experiences to provide the necessary stimulus for improvisation. Although the possible variations and mixtures of feelings are endless, these emotional states are probably the most difficult to work with because they are the least easy to objectify. Here is just a brief sample of emotions that might stimulate improvisation.

Aggressive	Desperate	Majestic
Amorous	Flippant	Obsessed
Angry	Forlorn	Pensive
Attentive	Frenetic	Pompous
Benevolent	Gloomy	Proud
Bored	Greedy	Shy
Compulsive	Haughty	Silly
Conniving	Humble	Sly
Delirious	Indignant	Sneaky
Desirous	Irresponsible	Victorious

Motor Stimuli

The sensing of some of the following physical actions produced either by the body itself or by forces outside the body may stimulate dance improvisation:

Bouncing	Exploding	Growing
Bumping	Flying	Jerking
Crowding	Fleeing	Pulsating
Disintegrating	Floating	Revolving
Elevating	Gliding	Rocking
Evolving	Going and coming	Rolling

Rotating	Speeding	Tilting
Shrinking	Spinning	Tumbling
Sliding	Starting and stopping	Undulating
Slithering	Swaying	Vibrating
Soaring	Thrusting	Withering

Physical Qualities, Shapes, and Textures

One might improvise to images of combinations of two or more of the following:

Angular	Hard	Slippery
Asymmetrical	Linear	Smooth
Bulbous	Liquid	Soft
Circular	Pendular	Sticky
Cylindrical	Rough	Symmetrical
Dense	Round	Tense
Elastic	Scraggly	Tough
Flat	Sharp	Winding
Fluffy	Sinewy	

Concepts and Ideas

One may create situations or recall the essence of them for ideas, images, or concepts to be used as stimuli. Such ideas may be constructed from the following:

Alienation	Emergence	Interrelatedness
Confrontation	Evocation	Meeting and parting
Desire	Greed	Transition
Elegance	Indifference	

For added excitement and challenge one might combine stimuli from several of the various categories above, such as furniture, pompous, vibrate, and pendular.

The following suggestions should help students toward successful nonliteral improvisation:

1. Submerge oneself in the job to be done by total involvement with the stimulus and avoidance of planning intellectually.

2. Explore movements extensively in one position such as kneeling, and then try another position such as lying, squatting, sitting, or standing.

3. Transfer movements from one part of the body to another and adapt them by changing to a position in which the same movement cannot be performed.

4. Explore small segments of the body—wrists, neck, elbows, ankles; practice using them together and separately.

5. Try to shut out all distractions concentrating totally on movement sensation.

The improvisation problems that follow are listed alphabetically by subject and organized under separate headings as to subject stimulus. Many of these problems can be done either individually or in groups.

1. Curvilinear movement and motion

Problem: Move continuously in soft curved lines, relating all body parts to curved motion. Experiment with curved movement in arms, legs, torso, neck, pelvis in stationary position and in locomotion. Define the curve.

Accompaniment: Select recorded orchestral or string music that will stimulate a lyrical quality and a sense of flow. Follow the musical lines for phrasing of movement; then deliberately change the phrasing by moving in short measures or elongated measures that overlap the phrasing suggested by the music.

Value: Sensing of curvilinear; awareness of movement phrasing apart from the musical stimulus: exploration of lyrical movement.

2. Development of movement theme

Problem: Improvise themes using movement as a subject and rehearse until they form a set sequence. Select some of the better themes and have the composer of each teach his theme to a group of three or four other students. Have the group then improvise on this theme and rehearse the improvisation until it takes on a definite form and sequence. All development should be intuitive and there should be no discussion.

Accompaniment: Accompaniment can be added after the improvisation takes a form. None should be used during the exploration unless the accompanist is improvising on what the dancers are doing.

Value: Experience in improvising a theme individually and in groups.

3. Emotional qualities in abstract form

Problem: Identify a situation in which emotions are strong. Extract from that situation a particular emotional state and analyze its component factors. Then, ignoring the context of the original situation, use these factors as motivation for movement improvisation.

Accompaniment: None.

Value: Experience in conceiving neuromuscularly from abstract motivation.

4. Free association

Problem: Select a subject, such as sailing, snow, cybernetics, rituals, parenthood. Take any phase of the subject and improvise from it allowing movements to unfold spontaneously. Let new ideas or feeling occur regardless of their relevance to the original subject. The student should constantly be aware of exactly how he is moving and where he is spatially and he should try to remember the feeling of the movement, its form, shape, and its flow of energy.

Accompaniment: None.

Value: Sensitizing the body for improved articulation and freer motivation.

5. Metric and nonmetric rhythm

Problem: Work in pairs with one student moving in metric rhythm, the other in nonmetric. Use an antiphonal form of statement and response with occasional overlapping of each other's movement. Then switch roles. Any idea or theme may be used as motivation but movement should be free of gesture and descriptive actions.

Accompaniment: Accompaniment, if used, can be either metric or nonmetric.

Value: Sensing movement in two rhythmic structures and the relationships that can occur between them.

6. Impulsion

Problem: Start with any part of the body, such as the sternum. Move the sternum forward on an impulse and then return. Avoid forcing it muscularly—let it move as a result of internal motivation as though the movement were involuntary. Repeat the action many times, carrying the initial impulse into other parts of the body to create additional motion by impulse. Explore as many body leads as possible; then make two different impulses occur together and allow the resultant movement to travel to other parts of the body.

Accompaniment: None.

Value: Experiencing a new way of moving; identifying specific areas of the body for initiation and control of movement impulses.

7. Motional interaction

Problem: Enact a drama of interacting motion between two or three people. Improvise movement and motion with special attention to timing and ways of articulating movement with each other. Use themes of relationship, such as alienation or interdependence of group, avoiding literal gestures and emotional overtones. Achieve the result by proximity, body and movement relationships, timing. The resultant improvisation can be either serious or humorous.

Accompaniment: None unless accompanist follows students.

Value: Experiencing dance in an abstract dramatic form.

8. Movement and music relationships

Problem: Do the following three exercises separately:

a. Move in direct response to music, exactly imitating the rhythm.

b. Now move in direct opposition to the music (moving slowly when music is fast and quickly when it is slow, move during musical pauses, and pause when the music is in progress).

c. Move with music as general background without regard for its phrasing or dynamics and responding only to its mood or theme.

Accompaniment: Select music from recordings in last section of this book, or use any available music that is appropriate to the problem.

Value: Awareness of musical phrasing versus movement phrasing; experiencing different movement and music relationships.

9. Phrase timing

Problem: Improvise movement sequences of varying lengths. Begin with a movement impulse and develop it intuitively, pausing when it is completed. Start a new impulse and do the same thing. Some phrases will be short and some longer; allow the movement to determine its own phrasing. Attempt to do the same thing in pairs and in small groups.

Accompaniment: None.

Value: Sensing of relative time values in movement.

10. Physical qualities

Problem: Create movement phrases by improvising around one of the following qualities of motion: undulation, explosion, pulsation, vibration, sway, inflation, deflation, sinking, disintegration, gliding. After the phrases are set, vary them by degrees of timing, for example, from quick to slow undulation or from inflation to deflation.

Accompaniment: None.

Value: Developing a highly differentiated concept of quality of motion.

11. Reactions to situations

Problem: Design situations such as the following to use as stimuli for improvisation:

    a. Inherited a million
    b. Flunked exams
    c. First cruise
    d. Visiting outer space
    e. Getting lost in the museum of natural history
    f. Crowds

The emphasis is on the student's response to a situation as he conceives it from the verbal presentation. The improvisation should be based on motivated feeling that is reiterated in a number of ways. Use movement design, motion, and essence of feeling as the materials of the improvisation. Do not allow much time to think about the idea before moving in response to it.

Accompaniment: None.

Value: Experience in responding nonliterally to literal situations.

12. Rhythm and movement

Problem: Use a variety of percussion instruments to establish a strong basic beat from which groups of from four to six students can improvise rhythmic movement patterns they create intuitively. Let some members of each group play the instruments while others move to rhythmic figures played.

Accompaniment: Percussion.

Value: Sensing the structured relationship of rhythmic pulse and rhythmic patterns to a basic underlying beat.

13. Sensing movement relationships

Problem: Use movement of a partner as a stimulus. Improvise responses to each other's movements. Work for sensitive responses and awareness of one another and the chance relationships that occur. Utilize kinetic and kinesthetic cues as well as visual and spatial ones. Do not intellectualize or plan responses while moving.

Accompaniment: None.

Value: Experiencing and understanding the mechanics of the kinetic relationships between one's own movement and that of another person. Recognizing the relationship kinesthetically and visually by observing.

Developing Movement Sequences

The following materials are grouped by number and type so that one may start either by chance or by choice selection in developing a dance sequence. Regardless of how one begins, the sequence will inevitably be developed and fulfilled by the individual's intuitive selection and shaping. The approach presented here is not intended as a basic pattern to follow but rather as a means of starting movement invention and of shaking earlier preconceptions and prejudices. By including all factors, one may build a more interesting as well as more complex movement phrase, or one might aim for greater simplicity by limiting the number of factors.

The movement phrase will be constructed on a walking base progressing generally in a forward direction in space. One may use forms of locomotion other than walking in the development or variation of the sequence. To follow the chance beginning, randomly select a number from the ranges beside each of the letters below:

A. 1 through 3
B. 1 through 3
C. 1 through 18
D. 1 through 24
E. 1 through 23
F. 1 through 11
G. 6 through 15
H. 1 through 3
I. 1 through 5

These letters correspond to the following:

A. *Dimension*: 1) depth, 2) height, 3) width

B. *Level*: 1) high, 2) low, 3) medium

C. *Shape of movement*: 1) angular, 2) asymmetrical, 3) bulbous, 4) curved, 5) deep, 6) flat, 7) jagged, 8) long, 9) massive, 10) pointed, 11) round, 12) short, 13) spiral, 14) square, 15) symmetrical, 16) thick, 17) thin, 18) any combination of two shapes

D. *Quality or texture*: 1) billowy, 2) brittle, 3) dense, 4) elastic, 5) fast, 6) flimsy, 7) grotesque, 8) hard, 9) heavy, 10) jerky, 11) light, 12) linear, 13) lofty, 14) pendular, 15) percussive, 16) rigid, 17) shaky, 18) slow, 19) smooth-flowing, 20) soft, 21) still, 22) sustained, 23) vibratory, 24) wispy

E. *Type of action*: 1) arch, 2) bend, 3) bounce, 4) collapse, 5) curl, 6) drag, 7) elevate, 8) evolve, 9) expand, 10) explode, 11) glide, 12) lunge, 13) press, 14) pull, 15) pulsate, 16) push, 17) rebound, 18) rise, 19) rotate, 20) tilt, 21) tumble, 22) undulate, 23) vibrate

F. *Directions*: 1) forward, 2) backward, 3) sideward right, 4) sideward left, 5) diagonally forward right, 6) diagonally forward left, 7) diagonally backward right, 8) diagonally backward left, 9) up, 10) down, 11) around.

G. *Time*: Length of phrase in counts, six through fifteen; Accents placed freely

H. *Size-range of movement*: 1) large, 2) medium, 3) small

I. *Intensity*: Pattern of energy release by degrees from 1 (least) to 5 (greatest)

Once one has his code, he then may translate it into specific requirements. For example, the code of A-1, B-1, C-11, D-13, E-15, F-4, G-7, H-1, I-3 would be translated into movement phrases requiring the following characteristics: depth dimension, high level, round shape, lofty quality, pulsating action, sideward left direction, seven counts, large in size, and moderate in intensity.

Using the above specifications as a sample problem, develop a movement sequence that meets all of the requirements. Although the requirements have been set by chance, the development of the movement will be the responsibility of the dancer—in other words, two or more persons doing the same problem should logically come up with different solutions. Should two factors conflict (such as high level and small range) they may be separated and performed on different beats of the measure or occur at the same time in different parts of the body. This becomes a really challenging problem in coordination, one well worthy of pursuing. Avoid the common tendency to crowd everything into a short number of beats and simply walk the rest of the time. Encourage repetition in at least part of the movement and urge that movement occur throughout the phrase to develop skill and control.

Developing a Phrase

Now that the unit of a measure or two is developed, the problem is to make it grow into a phrase. A phrase can be of any length that allows for the contour or shape of movement to be fulfilled. For example, if we have a seven count measure of movement that needs to be repeated in part, and the repetition consumes five of the seven counts, we can hold the remaining two counts; we now have phrase A which consists of two measures of seven. The movement determines the phrasing requirements. The requirements of the second phrase, B, may be the same, shorter or longer, depending on the movement and the individual. The movement may contain a further development of some of the material in A; it may also introduce some new material with that selected from A; or it may present material contrasting to A. The third phrase, C, will depend on A and B and the person developing it. Thus, phrases are built and developed around a central core of movement proceeding intuitively on a kind of theme and variations or theme and development scheme. The difference from the theme and variation technique is that new material may be introduced either with the old material or completely apart from it if it "feels right" and is kinetically logical and justifiable in relation to the source or motivation of the dance.

When enough phrases have been developed and hold together as a unified whole, we have developed a dance. The dance may range from very short to very long depending on the material itself and the conception of the choreographer—traditional rules of phrasing do not apply to nonliteral dance. The structure of the dance is developed to suit the material of the dance, the motivation from which it derives, and the individuality of the choreographer. Instead of forcing material into a predetermined form, one lets the material dictate that form. Perhaps at this point the reader has concluded that this process of creating dance is simple. But it is far from that, requiring constant inventing, selecting, varying, articulating, weighing and judging movements, and disciplining the outcome to the source or core of motivation. All of these activities are based on many guiding principles which the dancer needs to understand and apply. For a discussion of these principles the reader is referred to chapter 4.

Dance Problems

The following problems in nonliteral choreography place special emphasis on individuality, directness of expression, and clarity of communication. Although each problem is designed to develop a specific choreographic skill, it includes auxiliary skills as well.

The purpose of this section on problems is to present problems whose solutions will result in short dances worthy of developing. Some of the problems might constitute a semester's or a year's work, depending on the instructor's ingenuity and the student's readiness to tackle problems in depth. One can readily adapt these problems to suit his individual needs—whether a mere acquaintance with the subject of dance or a solid foundation with constant drill and practice. The problems can be assigned to individuals or groups, and even though they are designed and packaged, they can be redesigned and reused in a variety of different ways.

In evaluating the solutions to these problems, the teacher should use the criteria of structure, form, communicative value, and kinetic appropriateness. As he observes the results of his students' creative attempts and helps them criticize their work, the teacher should be absorbing new insights and growing with his class.

Listed alphabetically by subject, the examples state the problem and how it is to be presented, and the objective(s) or benefit(s) to be derived from its solution.

1. Alive-Stillness

Problem: Develop a short dance study of four or five phrases based on the quality of stillness: practice being still in various stationary positions (sitting, kneeling, standing) but with the potential of imminent movement. Sense the aliveness of body suspension upward and outward from its center in the various directions indicated by the position. At the point where the impulse to move becomes imperative, allow movement to take place slowly; complete the sequence or phrase and arrive at another position and pause. Repeat this process from the beginning until a form or pattern evolves. Motion should appear effortless and spontaneous.

Objective: To experience potential movement and allow it freedom to evolve and take shape. To awaken sensitivity to contrasts of stillness and motion and develop ability to remain stationary in an active way.

2. Articulation of movement and motion

Problem: Teach the students five different measures of movement that possess contrast in direction, quality, dimension, and level. Then ask them to find an appropriate order for these measures, allowing them to use any additional connecting movement that will lend shape, quality, timing, and continuity to the finished phrase.

Objective: To emphasize the importance of continuity between units of movement and gain practical experience in connecting movement sequences; to think in terms of the dynamics of phrasing.

3. Body Limitations

Problem: Explore exhaustively the many ways in which the following may be used: 1) joints of the body, 2) hands, 3) legs, 4) head, 5) torso.

Objective: To provide practice in slight variation of movement and to discover the immense variety of movement and motion that is possible in various parts of the body; to experience new ways of moving.

4. Body leads

Problem: Initiating impulses to move by various parts of the body:

a. Lying relaxed on back, isolate the following movements by lifting: right shoulder, nose, chin, chest, left shoulder, knees, hips. Roll to one side and do the same with free hip, free shoulder, and head. Lying face down, do the same with lower back, hips, upper back, neck, etc.

b. Lying on back, adjust position as required to move two parts together such as left hip and right shoulder or sternum and right knee. Explore unusual combinations. Try three body parts together.

c. With a walking base and traveling forward, use a single body lead employing shoulders, hips, side, head, etc. Then alternate two body leads, changing from one to the other on specific counts. Build a measure or two that requires many parts to be used in a complex timing pattern.

d. Emphasize the need to avoid compensatory movements. Make the lead appear free of other movements and body tensions unrelated to the intended action.

Objective: To increase awareness of the many areas of the body and to learn how to impel the body into motion by initiating movement from these areas. To increase coordination and control of body parts and stimulate more complex and interesting movements that one would not naturally discover on his own.

5. Clarity of statement

Problem: Extend the arm forward and return to starting position. Repeat in the most direct manner possible with no compensatory biases in body position or tensions. Concentrate on this single act alone. Repeat this forward extension using the feet, legs, body, head, and both arms together. Aim for the simplest statement possible. Develop a kinetically integrated sequence of such simple statements, achieving dynamics through contrast of direction, level, and time.

Objective: To increase simplicity, directness, and clarity of movement; to develop a sense of linear purity and kinesthetic awareness of the body design in a spatial context.

6. Communication through movement and motion

Problem: Create a dance study that communicates mainly through movement and motion. One may use idea, style, or mood as motivation but not images, symbols, gestures, emotionalism, or anything that becomes representative or that requires translation.

Objective: To experience the purity of movement and motion as a communication vehicle.

7. Complex and detailed movement

Problem: Create a short dance study based on a style or mood and consisting of simple structure, clear line, and movement variety. Use as much detail within that structure as it can support. To assure the complexity of the movement, manipulate and use all of the smaller segments of the body, irregular rhythms, asymmetry, and variety in direction and level.

Objective: To develop the use of smaller joint actions in the body and to become aware of detail in movement sequence; to challenge one's coordination abilities and thereby develop better neuromuscular control; to sense the residual motion that results from many quick movements.

8. Design and motion

Problem: Build a series of five to eight designs based on one of the following shapes or qualities: symmetrical, asymmetrical, grotesque, linear, circular, soft, hard. Develop motional transitions appropriate to the quality of the design. Perform the sequence two ways, 1) by giving dominance to the design, and 2) by giving dominance to the motional factors. Compare the differences in total effect.

Objective: To identify the choreographic elements at work in the interrelationship of body, motion, and design; to become aware of these elements separately and together.

9. Dynamic motional interaction

Problem: Working alone, start by moving one part of the body and react to this movement with another part of the body; establish a chain of spontaneous reactions that feel appropriately timed.

a. Work with a partner in alternating actions as well as in overlapping movement responses.

b. Do the same in groups of three and four.

Objective: To experience and practice making the body responsive to one's own movement and that of others; to tune the body to a higher pitch of kinetic excitement and interaction.

10. Dynamic phrase

Problem: Walk to a steady basic beat and think in terms of a phrase of twelve counts. Class members will then place a movement lasting three counts somewhere within the twelve, set it, and practice it. Once everyone has set his movement, add the following,

one at a time, mastering each before moving on to the next. Each
addition should be maintained as new ones are added.

    a. An accent in two places

    b. A movement diagonally forward and upward

    c. A movement diagonally backward

    d. A low movement

    e. A turn

    f. Elevation

    g. A pronounced rhythmic pattern in the feet

When the phrase is completed, it should be practiced to refine
the structure, timing, volume, and shape necessary for kinetic fulfillment of the movement phrase.

Objective: To build a dynamic phrase and fulfill it in terms of the
interrelationship of its movement-motion elements.

11. Imagery

Problem: Identify and define an image concerned with an action
such as floating, withering, soaring, evolving, revolving, crowding,
slithering. Create the feeling of the chosen image in movement that
is unrelated to anything concrete. Develop the movement theme;
create variations on it by selecting parts to be developed into movement phrases. Organize and develop the dance using the best arrangement of variations.

Objective: To explore imagery as a thematic source for nonliteral
choreography.

12. Kinetic evolvement

Problem: Start with a given motor impulse. Let it develop and
go where it is inclined to go. Add to or change it when it feels intuitively right to do so. The impulse to move should originate from
the torso and travel outward through the extremities. Avoid intellectual planning to attain the greatest spontaneity and inventiveness.
Let each movement stimulate the next.

Objective: To explore kinetic logic; to learn to move kinetically and to develop a movement to conclusion; to develop awareness of the complexity of movement; to create movement phrases with gradual transitions.

13. Life events

Problem: Observe life processes directly as they occur; for example, a baby learning to stand or walk, a puppy frisking, ants building a hill, a plant breaking ground. Select one process, extract the essential form of its action, and use this form with an imposed but appropriate idea, image, or theme for a dance. First the movement should be developed from the basic quality of the process, its shape, character, and texture. Once the movement is established an appropriate image should be sought to be superimposed on it.

Objective: To relate basic forms of life to movement through direct experience and to use their designs deliberately.

14. Literal sources of nonliteral dance

Problem: Develop a pantomime based on some daily activity or sport. Analyze the movement in terms of its design characteristics. Begin by using the movement's pattern and form as the movement theme. Treat the movement theme as content apart from its source—experiment with timing, dynamics, and motional values of the movement phrase. Repeat parts of the action or vary it for special dynamic effects. Develop the phrase as a movement theme for its own sake.

Objective: To relate the differences between literal and nonliteral conception and treatment of movement materials and form.

15. Motion as content and communication

Problem: Compose a dance study that uses motion as its subject matter. The communicated result in this study should be achieved primarily through motion. No other thematic material is necessary. Work intuitively rather than intellectually, eliminating gesture and emotionalism. The structure of motion should become integrated around a central core of movement that possesses strong motional value.

Objective: To focus on motion as the principle vehicle of communication.

16. Movement invention

Problem: Compose a dance study consisting entirely of unusual movement. Use angular, curved, and linear shapes or select an image to communicate such as scraggly, rough, smooth. Create movement that uses all parts of the body independently as opposed to paired parallel, or oppositional use of arms and legs. Consider all parts of the body as possible combinations with all other parts. Make unusual combinations.

Objective: To shake habitual patterns of natural movement and discover many new ways of moving to create movement that exists for its own sake, that is, inventive, unusual, unique in design, quality, sequence, and timing.

17. Movement and music relationships

Problem: Select one of the following:

a. Start with a recorded musical selection that is full, intricate, and elaborate. Weave an appropriate theme to this music, making the movement as simple and uncomplicated as possible.

b. Take a simple piece of music and weave around it a dominant theme with complex and detailed movement.

c. Develop a dance study without music; select a contrasting piece of music as accompaniment for the completed study.

Objective: To explore various relationships of dance to music.

18. Movement shapes

Problem: Assume a series of body positions that are round; then do several that are flat, pointed, thin, irregular, deep, thick, massive, curved, jagged, long. Select one shape and give it a particular degree of weight ranging somewhere between heavy and light. Create movement variations on this position, exhausting all the possibilities within the problem and avoiding the introduction of new or contrasting materials.

Objective: To practice developing a limited amount of material and to develop sensitivity to movement shapes and quality as materials of dance.

19. Movement theme

Problem: Create a dance study around a central movement theme (pulsation, angularity, or some specific quality as content). Determine what is kinetically logical and what is not. Select examples from student works and analyze what makes movement kinetically logical or illogical in each; study both in regard to movement articulation and relation of movement development to theme.

Objective: To sense the relationship of movement development to a central movement theme apart from intellectual logic. To sharpen aesthetic sensitivity.

20. Nonliteral use of emotion

Problem: Select a particular feeling (such as amorous, benevolent, conniving, desirous, forlorn, humble, irresponsible, obsessed, victorious); analyze and list its basic components. Use these characteristics as sources for creating movement and developing the form of the dance. This problem is not concerned with a person in the act of feeling emotions, but with emotion itself as the content of the dance; therefore, avoid dramatic gesture.

Objective: To develop the ability to conceive neuromuscularly from an abstract concept; to explore emotion as subject matter of a nonliteral dance composition.

21. Objects and movement

Problem: Design or find an object that can be used as an extension of the body. A suitable object might be one of the following:

elastic tapes, stretch fabric, boxes—all shapes, drums, stools, tissue paper, coat and hat pole, percussion instruments. Explore the object's shape, texture, design, and basic nature. Improvise with it until appropriate movement evolves. Develop the image or movement theme with the object, allowing the movement to take shape intuitively. Remember not to impose form but to let it happen.

Objective: To experience the transition from concrete object to abstract movement; to heighten sensitivity to an object's texture, shape, and quality and their relationship to movement and motion.

22. Objects as sources of dance content

Problem: List a number of objects on the blackboard, such as diamond, rock, venetian blind, reclining chair, stairs. Select one object and identify its characteristic shape, texture, color, and form. The diamond, for example, is faceted in shape and many-sided; its texture is smooth, sharp-edged, and hard; its color is white but transparent, reflecting, and brilliant; its form is solid. Select from the listed characteristics at least one from each category and use them as the subject of dance movement without referring to the original source for association. Use the most dominant characteristic as the central core around which the movement quality of the dance is created.

Objective: To experience one process by which one moves into the nonliteral realm of choreography.

23. Physical qualities of motion

Problem: Develop a movement phrase based on physical qualities of motion such as undulating, pulsating, vibrating, disintegrating, swaying, rolling, sliding. Use one quality as the content of a study, being careful to avoid imitation of objects or people who perform these physical motions. In other words, employ the qualities of motion as entities apart from their association with literal sources.

Objective: To explore physical qualities of motion for their innate characteristics and as a means of creating inventive nonliteral movement.

24. Poetic Imagery

Problem: Select a poem with vivid imagery; use the imagery as the content for a dance study. Avoid literal symbols or gestures for communication. Work specifically and intuitively with imagery as the source of movement invention. The poem can be used as accompaniment for the dance or the dance may be performed unaccompanied or to musical accompaniment.

Objective: To choreograph to images, allowing the movement to assume its own form and timing.

25. Projection

Problem: Develop a three-part study in which the first part contains extensive projection of movement from a stationary position into distant space. Part two should consist of movements from a stationary base to an area twelve feet away in space. Part three is to use extensive projection outward into space by actually traveling through space. Work for directness in addressing space as an entity.

Objective: To increase kinesthetic awareness of the process of movement projection and of controlled spatial dimensions.

26. Prologue

Problem: Design an introduction in movement to a specific television show. Use no gesture. Create atmosphere and a sense of what is to follow by using stylized movement, attitude or mood, group relationships and timing, motional dynamics.

Objective: To introduce a concrete subject nonliterally.

27. Space and motion

Problem: Design a study in space that creates certain illusions such as space that shrinks and expands, space that is endless, linear, massive, or thick. Select an image of spatial action as content. Dramatize the image motionally; engulf it, carve it, shape it, scatter it.

Objective: To explore the interrelationship of movement, motion, and space; to understand and appreciate the complexity of space as an entity in dance.

28. Spatial dimensions

Problem: Start from any sitting position; move arms and legs in two different dimensions (height, depth, width) and return to starting position. Sense the distance projected by movement. Intend the movement to be carried to a predetermined distance and intensify the movement to project that distance. Concentrate on extending movement into space. Then vary as follows:

a. Explore in the same way by assuming various shapes of movement, such as curved, square, linear, angular.

b. Explore in kneeling, standing, and the various positions used for pliés.

c. Take the shapes in *a* and carve them out of space in alternating height, depth, and width dimensions.

d. Repeat *c*, improvising while moving through space doing variations of one shape in many dimensions.

e. Set a sequence of shapes and give specific timing.

Objective: To increase awareness of the body as it moves in space; to achieve more complex and inventive movement having a specific spatial orientation.

29. Stylized movement

Problem: Develop a stylized study based on an image of one of the following movement qualities: angular, curved, linear, jittery, undulating, tense, vibrating. Vary the timing sharply. Analyze the specifics of the selected quality and deliberately design movement to produce that image. Do not introduce any movement foreign to the chosen quality.

Objective: To explore one style as intensively as possible.

30. Themes

Problem: Select a subject for a large general theme from among the following suggestions:

    a. Life: action, existence, affluence, seeing, feeling, thinking, developing, mating, individual, family, group

    b. Variegation: irridescent, mottled, checkered, spotted, mosaic, harlequin

    c. Loquacity: gabble, verbosity, gossip, small talk

Each group should take one phase of the same theme to develop.

Objective: To experience the relationship of nonliteral choreography to a central theme.

31. Timing and movement

Problem: Use the feeling of curiosity as the subject of a dance theme. Think through situations in which curiosity is strong, considering them from a child's point of view as well as an adult's. Extract from these situations the essence and characteristics of curiosity including timing and rhythmic pattern. These characteristics now become the dance subject. Using timing as the dominant vehicle of communication, try to convey the essence of curiosity.

Objective: To sense the importance of timing as an essential element of choreography.

Technique

Technique is concerned with the way a dance is performed. Good technique means not simply knowing the movements but understanding how movement relates to dance content. It implies a neuromuscular sophistication that grows out of many hours of hard work, of observation, analysis, and self-evaluation. And it involves self-discipline, control of the body, and awareness of the many complex components of movement and motion and their communication in the final performance.

Conditioning the body is just one of the training methods that contribute to good technique. It includes stretching the spine, flexing and extending the joints, strengthening various muscle groups and areas of the body, coordinating complex movement sequences, and exploring new ways to move. Its purpose is to mold the body into a flexible, strong, controlled, and agile instrument.

Learning the art of movement and motion in relation to space is another essential of technical skill. It can be achieved through the use of motor images that help the student discover movement and space relationships for himself. Because such relationships are not teachable entities, they must be created internally by the individual student.

A third way to improve technique is by performing difficult and challenging movement sequences that require the student to fulfill the shape, texture, and volume implied by the movement. These complex movement sequences demand that the dancer constantly integrate, coordinate, time, and refine movement.

Basic to the designing of dance problems that lead to technical skill is the isolation of common errors in technique. Their number is endless, but here are some of the most frequent:

1. Lack of spatial orientation of the body
2. Working for extremes beyond optimal degrees, such as the highest jump, the widest spread, the most tension
3. Lack of kinesthetic awareness
4. Casualness of performance—no sense of immediacy, no excitement or vibrancy
5. Tendency to settle into the body rather than stretch out of it
6. Poor continuity
7. Dropping of motion between positions
8. Failing to fulfill the shape and volume of movement

9. Conflicting tensions within the body
10. Excessive tensions
11. Incompatible movements
12. Inactive or overactive stillness on pauses
13. Resting at the ends of movement phrases
14. Idiosyncrasies leading to ambiguous cues
15. Inexact movement detail

The technique exercises given here are designed to help develop the wide range of skills that are essential to a polished perform- ance. To derive full benefit from them, the students must regard their creative efforts as laboratory specimens and be willing to per- form them for others to observe and analyze. The class should identify and discuss the technical principles[1] listed in chapter four in relation to their own work and the work of other students. These principles are guides rather than rules. They can also serve as standards for evaluating the finished product.

Technique problems

1. Have students improvise or set a) a series of quick, short movements separated by pauses, b) a series of positions with a pause following each, and c) a series of positions each separated by motion followed by pause. Give equal emphasis to movement, position, motion, and pause. Experiment freely with timing and rhythmic changes.

2. Teach the class a simple movement sequence that has several changes of direction and focus. Practice this phrase in order to state it with maximum directness. Avoid extraneous motivation and idiosyncrasies, such as affectations, head tilting, etc.

3. Start with a dynamic movement phrase, preferably one that

---

1. Margery J. Turner, "Non-literal Modern Dance—Its Nature, Forms and Means of Communication," *"Research Quarterly of the American Asso- ciation for Health, Physical Education and Recreation* 36, no. 1 (March 1965): 94.

has been developed in a previous class session. Practice the phrase to fulfill the volume of movement, refine the pattern of energy release, and clarify the linear and spatial design. Evaluate the strengths and deficiencies of the phrase.

4. Teach a series of four or five movements in a sequence. Have the students practice the sequence individually, performing each movement as though it were the first and most important of all. This entails relinquishing the preceding movement for the next and is an attempt to eliminate biases from previous movements. If each movement is performed fully and yields to the next in turn, the sequence will be performed with maximum clarity.

5. Select a section of a dance study that is familiar to the students. Practice performing it with a sense of urgency or attack, but keep it from being rushed.

6. Perform a simple movement that can be repeated constantly, such as rising to the toes and returning, undulating one arm, rocking back and forth. Perform the chosen movement, attempting to give the illusion of perpetual motion. Insert pauses of varying lengths at different points in the movement. Other than at the conclusion, allow the length of the pause to vary and begin again from the point where the pause occurred.

7. Build a long movement phrase that is unique, inventive, and of unnatural design. Develop the phrase spontaneously by having each movement evolve from the preceding one. After evaluating several of the students' phrases, select a well-designed sample and have the class watch successive performances of it, practicing it mentally while they watch. Then have them perform the movement phrase.

8. Have the students perform the following sequence: Reach in a right sideward direction as far as the hand will go and return to position; reach upward with the left hand and return; reach directly downward with the right hand and return to position. After the skeletal form of the movement is understood, have the students practice it by performing the same reaching movements in the most

direct manner possible with the head and eye focus paralleling hand movement. They may time the movement as they wish but they must keep the body as the initial motivating point from which the hand reaches. All peripheral action must bear a consistent relationship with the body if the movement is to be valid. Work for simplicity and directness of statement.

9. Group at least ten students within a twenty-square-foot area and, using any body lead, have them walk to a basic beat, taking care to avoid touching anyone; should a collision appear imminent, they are to change direction. Each change in direction should be accompanied by a corresponding change in movement idea. While approaching someone, they should try to convey a sense of relationship. Pauses may be used at random. Students may move in any direction and with different body leads. Directions should be accurately defined.

10. Use a movement phrase that the students have created previously. Perform it the way it was created and have the class identify its dynamics and texture. Gradually change the timing to increase or decrease speed. Have the class analyze the changes in dynamics and texture that result from the new timing. Discuss the effect of the timing change on the phrase as a whole.

11. Teach a sequence of at least five movements that have motivation. Have the students articulate them so that they constitute a whole phrase. Practice making each movement of the phrase important.

12. Teach a short but complex movement phrase by having the class observe and imitate it. Ask the class to identify as many of its elements as they can find. Observe their performance of the phrase. Contrast an accurate with an inaccurate performance and ask the students to name the missing elements. List as many elements as can be observed in order to emphasize the movement's complexity.

13. Select an object that moves, such as an animal, a natural force or a mechanical device. Analyze its action and rhythm. Re-

produce the same quality of motion and timing in movement. Refine the movement.

14. Create a variety of shapes by designing body parts into positions. Experiment by moving with these shapes and within them, and, at the same time, maintain the character of the movement design as well as fulfill its volume.

4

Principles of Nonliteral
Choreography

Basic Principles

Practice in solving problems of various types such as those in chapter three leads the student to experience and understand dance in its own terms. He develops an understanding of the choreographic process through value judgments, weighing and analyzing the uses of materials and techniques of dance as vehicles for communication. From these experiences he reaches for deeper understanding of the processes of movement expression and begins to build a total concept of dance choreography.

The purpose of this chapter is to present basic principles of dance choreography through conception of a model, a theoretical design of the factors of choreography and their interrelationships. Such theorizing is valuable in that it provides a structure to which one can relate experiences as well as test new ideas. Undoubtedly models vary from person to person, from one stage of development to another, and from one period of time to the next. Nevertheless, they provide a standard for evaluation of dance choreography as well as ideas one can challenge and test for validity.

The following model,[1] presented in outline form, suggests that

1. Margery J. Turner, "Non-literal Modern Dance—Its Nature, Forms and Means of Communication," *Research Quarterly of the American Association for Health, Physical Education and Recreation* 36, no. 1 (March 1965): 86–95.

there are three main factors of choreography,[2] the first of which is *content*. Dance choreography is a unique psychological and physical creation of the choreographer. It involves memory, past experience, value judgments, interaction of ideas, and probably what is most important, the original conception of the work. The psychological, physical, and spatial factors, while listed separately for purposes of analysis, are, in effect, all part of an integrated function resulting in movement that communicates artistically.

The second factor of nonliteral dance choreography is *form*, which structures, organizes, and orders the materials used.

The third factor is *technique*, which serves a disciplinary function. To achieve a technically skilled performance one must aim for simplicity, simultaneity, clarity, continuity, variety, conditioning, and integration.

The choreographer is concerned with the manipulation of content, form, and technique. He proceeds intuitively rather than with the aid of checklists or intellectual order. While he might use these factors to evaluate and analyze the finished product, he would not use them to choreograph in an analytical way.

The following elaboration of the principles of choreography is presented as a guide to the choreographic process:

  I. *Content* (sources): The communicated experience should be able to be sensed directly by the observer and it should make sense as an entity. To achieve these ends the choreographer must coordinate the functions of his mind and body.

    A. *Psychological* (motivation): The mental processes are the creative core of the dance. They involve the integrating of the intellectual, sensory, and emotional experiences for the purpose of selecting aesthetically appropriate movements (for specific psychological functions and qualities, see chapter two).

2. The factors of choreography are identified in relation to nonliteral dance. Some of these factors may or may not apply to traditional modern dance or to other forms of dance.

B. *Physical* (movement-motion): The body produces movement and motion in response to given motivation. The resultant movement must transcend mere muscular tension and at the same time remain disciplined to the demands of form (for specific functions and qualities of the physical, see chapter two).

C. *Spatial* (orientation): The dancer must be kinetically aware of movement and motion as they exist within a spatial constellation. All motion must be defined and refined in terms of its spatial components.

II. *Form* (organization): Form results when well-motivated motion evolves organically according to the following criteria:

A. *Spatial design*: Design includes the following elements: symmetry, asymmetry, balance, shape, line, texture, and volume. The choreographer must be constantly aware of dynamic line in multidimensional positions and of motion in space.

B. *Style* (movement type): The unique character of a dance is its style. This may be one which has existed before or it may be the unique creation of the choreographer. In either case the content of the dance must be appropriate to the movement style.

C. *Time* (organizing factor): The particular distribution of movement-motion energy in space involves factors of accent, duration, contrast, meter or nonmeter, phrase, pulse, tempo. It should be fulfilled for each movement.

D. *Development*: As a dance unfolds, its statement should expand. This expansion or development should be guided by kinetic feeling and motional logic, each movement evolving from the preceding one to produce an interrelated whole. The skillful choreographer can invent exciting new ways for motion to flow logically.

III. *Technique* (discipline): The same principles that guide choreographers in producing a well-constructed dance can be used

as criteria for evaluating the finished product. The following
principles relate directly to the process of dancing:

A. Personal idiosyncrasies as well as all superfluous material
   and decor should be eliminated.

B. The dancer should communicate directly using well-defined
   movement and motion as his vehicles. Motivation and motion should occur simultaneously to provide direct communication and eliminate accidental cues that lead to
   audience misinterpretation.

C. Once a movement is stated, the interplay of its shape, balance, relationship of time-motion dynamics and texture
   must be ongoing.

D. Degrees of change and contrast should be produced by
   manipulating and adding movements to create phrases of
   varying inventiveness and complexity.

E. Motion should be consistently related to the movement
   theme to produce a dance that has organic and structural
   unity. The dancer must be constantly aware of the totality
   of motional factors and of their multiplicity of detail in his
   effort to fulfill each movement within its timing structure.

F. Highly developed muscular sensitivity and control should
   be achieved by extensive practice and experimentation using all of the components of dance in their many forms and
   combinations. Continuous dance practice with motivation
   and understanding refines kinesthetic and kinetic awareness and develops control, thus freeing the body to become
   an expressive instrument.

Preparing Dances for Performance

The nonliteral choreographer can consider almost anything as
possible subject matter—he may choose a theme from the vast
realm of nature, or perhaps he might select a broad subject such
as war, death, or human relationships. Content may be animate or

inanimate, emotional or physical, attitudinal or situational. Ideas may range from very large to very small. Whatever his source, he transforms it into designed, inventive, and communicative movement through the use of basic materials of dance.

Student choreography does not just happen; it is preceded by considerable class experience in creative exploration of movement, technique, and compositional problem-solving. The most successful group choreography is produced when the students work under a teacher's imaginative yet unobstrusive guidance. Working independently the students can sense directly what they can and cannot perform well. But they need the expert direction of the teacher whose experience enables him to grasp their overall problems and who can, therefore, help them to set realistic goals.

Here is one way that a skillful teacher can help his students produce a polished dance suite suitable for performance. He sets the class to work solving a problem individually but using the same music. From the excellent themes that will emerge, he selects the best, organizes the class into various sized groups, and assigns each choreographer whose work was selected to one of the groups. Each group then learns one selected theme, refines it, and adapts it to the group with the help of the group. The resultant dance suite will reflect the students' exploration of contrasting themes.

Provision should be made for presentation of the finished work, either as part of an informal studio program with an invited audience or as a more formal dance recital. Although performance of finished dances should be a regular part of the learning experience, class work should never be determined by the school's performance needs.

How the Teacher Helps Evaluate

The process of evaluating student choreography appears to be a problem for young teachers, especially those attempting to foster creativity in a permissive atmosphere. They worry that if they do not accept student efforts without reservation, the students will lose creative initiative. Afraid of imposing their own ideas on their students, these teachers choose to remain too much in the background, refraining from making even routine criticisms or suggestions.

The inexperienced teacher can avoid the pitfalls of authoritarianism, however, if he remembers that the evaluation can be subtle and almost imperceptible when introduced at the very beginning of the class experiment. The stage for evaluation is set the moment a problem is presented.

The teacher's role in the evaluative process is to challenge the student's thinking and deepen his perceptions by asking him first to identify his own area of strength and weakness. The teacher then helps the student explore the possible reasons for these and questions the student in such a way that he, on his own, will discover and evaluate appropriate changes in his approach.

The teacher's role, then, is to stimulate the student to define and clarify his aesthetic and intellectual values. By serving as a kind of creative gadfly, he can launch the student along the path of self-discovery and thoughtful decision-making. And with the evaluation approached as a student-centered activity, it becomes a class experience in group dynamics, with the teacher frequently learning as much as the students.

To help students develop their full potential as dancers, choreographers, and spectators, the class should be considered a laboratory for learning. Students should be encouraged to experiment, test, analyze, and evaluate the results of their work. In such an experimental environment students can participate openly and without inhibitions, free to make their own exciting discoveries.

Evaluating nonliteral choreography is far more illusive and difficult than working with the more literal forms of dance. Nonliteral choreography presents neither a specific message, a dramatic form, nor representative gestures that one can discuss readily; one cannot apply intellectual logic in criticizing it. The work should be perceived then as a unity or totality. To determine the internal integrity in the use of dance materials, one must be absolutely clear about what he is doing and make use of his material in such a way that an organic existence is assured.

Clarity of communication, then, is a prime value. It can be achieved only when the dancer's conception, creation, and performance are organically interrelated. "It is only when all factors of an image, all their individual effects, are completely attuned to the one intrinsic vital feeling that is expressed in the whole—when, so to speak, the clarity of the image coincides with the clarity of the inner content—that a truly artistic form is achieved."[3]

Suggested Guide to Dance Evaluation

Besides the importance of clarity, many other aesthetic attributes are essential to effective dance communication. The following questions are suggested as guides to evaluation of nonliteral dance.

1. Does the dance hold together as an integrated whole?

2. Does the dance hold one's interest throughout? If so, why? If not, what was lacking?

3. Is the intention of the dance communicated clearly? How was it achieved? How can it be improved?

4. Is the movement inventive? Why or why not? Is it appropriate to the motivation?

5. Are vital movement components missing? Identify them. Are there materials included that are superfluous? Identify them.

6. Is there an apparent rhythmic organization? Does it aid communication?

7. Was the problem effectively solved?

8. Was the quality and kind of movement an effective solution to the problem? Why or why not? If not, what might be a good substitute?

3. Paul Stern, "On the Problems of Artistic Form," in *Reflections on Art*, ed. Susanne Langer (Baltimore: Johns Hopkins Press, 1958), p. 75.

9. Is there an element of surprise or can you anticipate each movement?

10. Did you see movement relationships that were new to you?

In guiding the discussion that will follow the questions, the teacher should bear in mind that it is not necessary to draw specific conclusions. Since there are no rules of choreography or final and definitive answers to questions raised, there can be no firm conclusion growing out of such class discussions. The suggested questions are intended rather to challenge students to think, explore, and examine. The common ideas and acceptances that may grow out of such an evaluation should in no way reflect any preconceptions or prejudices on the part of the teacher.

Music and Dance

The Use of Music for Dance

The essential artistic validity of the assumption that dance must be combined with music is open to question; however, one must recognize that dance and music are combined, through usage if not through artistic inevitability. It has yet to be shown that the connection between the two arts is other than that it has always been that way. The *tradition* of interdependence and the sources of influences shared by both arts constitute the major part of our understanding of their relatedness since there has been in no sense a development or evolution of either the technical or the idealistic possibilities inherent in the combination.

The purpose of this chapter is to explore briefly the sources of correlation between music and dance, and to encourage the dancer to develop a fundamental knowledge of rhythmic materials, structure, and notational symbols in order that he may be technically equipped to explore in great detail the only real formal characteristic that the two arts share—the organizing or unfolding of events in time. From the outset the reader must be aware that in the presentation of this material a distinction is made between two concepts in the utilization of music for dance: 1) music for the creation of a dramatic[1] or theater piece or as the basis of improvisational experiments and 2) rhythmic materials drawn from mus-

1. I use the word *dramatic* here to refer to any formal structure.

ical sources as support in the study of dance technique. While in past practice there has seemed to be no fixed boundary line, a clear understanding of the functional difference between the two concepts should aid the dancer in selecting the materials appropriate to his specific needs.

Metric Coordination

A dancer may select a piece of music because, besides being suitable for other reasons, it corresponds exactly in length to the dance conception. An unfortunate aspect of this problem of selection is that it is more difficult than it might seem at first glance to find a piece that will satisfy every purpose including the condition of equal total length. Consequently, there is a widespread theory that the music may be altered to accommodate the dance in terms of length or that sections of music may be freely shuffled, omitted, or repeated to suit the needs of the dance. It should serve as sufficient warning to the dancer to carefully consider the following: that it is in the dancer's best interests that the artistic integrity of any part of his creation be unimpaired, and, for the moment, the dancer does not usually have enough musical experience or background to estimate the subtle psychological damage done to the whole by a seemingly harmless mutilation of the musical part. With the vast quantity of recorded and published music available and the number of practicing musicians and composers who would be happy to consult with dancers on realistic problems such as the one in question, an artistically sound solution should always be possible.

A situation might easily be imagined, however, in which the music is totally incidental to the dance. In this case, we may safely assume that the dance may exist totally independent of the music and would be the same and communicate the same whether or not that music were present; hence there can be no practical objection to altering the music for convenience or even to achieve some theatrical effect. It should be noted that the prime reason that the dancer may require incidental music is to provide himself with cues that would insure his timing. Music that is used thus incidentally should not be depended upon to contribute anything essential to the dance, lest it call too much attention to itself and, if there have been alterations made, jeopardize the feeling of the whole. The ultimate success rests, therefore, on the accuracy of the dancer's judgment of precisely what *function* the music has in relation to the dance.

A dancer may select a piece of music for its metric structure and the possibilities that it presents for coordinating that metric structure with the metric structure of the movement concept as it exists or as it is to be realized. The primary consideration for selecting music on this basis is that the dancer may avail himself of rhythmic support in technical execution or an extra degree of rhythmic emphasis as it is needed.

In this metric structure is an exceedingly rich source of correlation, the surface of which has hardly been scratched. The creative limitations of the dancer in this area reflect sadly his lack of training in the specific materials of rhythm. It is not clear just why dancers have not felt the need to learn at least as much as the average musician must learn about rhythm. Rhythm is, after all, not the exclusive province of music but of any art form that projects ideas through the time medium, especially considering the dancer's constant use of, and tremendous reliance on, the tools and elements of rhythm. It is perhaps simply a matter of neglect through ignorance—a historically perpetuated ignorance of how valuable a knowledge of rhythm would be as a creative, technical, and instructive tool.

It cannot be emphasized too strongly that even the dancer's working definition of the rhythmic sense—that is, that a sense of rhythm consists of the ability to count "regularly" and to be able to *respond* with some degree of accuracy to outside rhythmic stimuli—inhibits its efficient use as a most important facet of his technical equipment. It must be remembered that creativity or the projection of an idea (including movement idea), though perhaps emanating from the senses, must ultimately be generated through the mind; the knowledge of raw materials is the food of that generative force.

Therefore, a more useful definition might be: a sense of rhythm is that sense which enables one to generate and project ideas by means of properties peculiar to the organization of events in time and to give cohesion to events in time by means of rhythmic articulation.

Though ultimately we must always return to the subject of rhythm as the most important source material for the development of some musical-kinetic relationship or idea, we may yet profitably return to examine some other aspects of the connections between music and dance.

The "Atmospheric" Condition

Another basis for selection might be called the "atmospheric" condition and may be defined simply as a correspondence of general mood or character between the dance and the music. This must be considered entirely a condition of individual subjective response, since, the nature of music being inherently abstract, any given piece of music will not necessarily elicit from every individual the same response. For an improvisation, therefore, the dancer may rely on the atmosphere of the music as a sole musical motivation, but in the creation of a piece for an audience, it is doubtful whether the correspondence of mood between dance and music as the *only* source of correlation will create for the spectator an experience of intrinsic artistic merit.

In utilizing the atmospheric condition it should be noted also that varying degrees of tension may be obtained through the judicious use of diametrically opposed moods, one against the other. The areas in between, however, tend to be dangerous (though not impossible) because they often describe nothing more than the fact that at this point the music and dance are not related, and an acute awareness of this on the part of the observer might precipitate an unwanted distraction of his attention.

Neither metric nor atmospheric motivations by themselves can be depended upon to culminate in a unique expression of music and dance; yet an intermingling or constantly shifting emphasis upon one or the other will certainly provide a fertile basis for the creation of that unique form.

One common basis for the selection of material, the matching or evocation of a particular style, is so highly spurious and productive of such incredibly uninteresting results as to be unworthy of consideration here. It is particularly distressing because it inhibits the use of music that might otherwise be enormously advantageous to the dancer. Style, in any art form, should be a matter of perspective gained with the passing of time and not an a priori consideration in the creation of that art.

Musical Gesture

A simple device, rich in artistic potential when sparingly and appropriately employed, is the visual representation of a musical gesture. Lest this practice degenerate to the level of mimicry (also referred to as "mickey-mousing"), it would be better to bear in mind as an ideal the fulfillment of the musical gesture rather than the imitation of it. Conversely, it may also be a gratifying experience to allow the music to fulfill the movement gesture on occasion, thus adding greatly to the vocabulary of interplay between dance and music.

The Adaptation of Musical Forms

Attempting to make a dance form out of a fugue, for example, simply by using a fugue as an accompaniment and imitating its most superficial aspects is perhaps as futile an endeavor as attempting to "express" a piece of music that is by itself its own expression. No one can seriously believe that dancing to a Bach fugue will in the least benefit or express the music and it is a matter of conjecture whether the music will in the least benefit the dance, insofar as it is not covering up a poverty of conception or lack of technique. If, however, we are dealing with a rearticulation in dance form of the materials of the fugue, then the technical details, the contrapuntal and harmonic unfolding of the complex formal structure, must be *redefined* in terms of the special properties of physical space, movement and design—all visual aspects that have nothing to do with the actual musical form of the fugue. When the transference of a concept can be made from the one language to the other, the dancer may legitimately claim to have been inspired by music. The more one knows about musical forms, then, the more successfully one can borrow from musical materials and, in certain contexts, even preclude the physical presence of that music as accompaniment.

Musical Materials

The musical materials available to the dancer today through recordings are extensive. For general use music that provides simple metric designs, such as some of the music of Vivaldi, Corelli—and on the more modern end of the scale—Bartok, and Webern, where much of the prime interest of the music is in the unfolding of these metric designs, will lend itself excellently to experimentation in the area of atmospheric as well as metric coordination. On the other hand, the music of Mozart, Bach, Beethoven, Schoenberg, and Stravinsky—to mention some obvious examples—does not easily lend itself to general use, the rhythmic structures being more subtly derived, consequently much more difficult to work with. In addition, most nineteenth century music, and to some extent American music of the first half of the twentieth century, presents a problem for the dancer as it does for the musician in relating it to contemporary life and its expressive needs. This is not to say categorically that this music may not be a successful source of material for the dancer. The difficulty lies, not in the merit of the music, which is no more questionable than the music of any other period, but in the inevitable associations which the music evokes. We must remember that the nineteenth century belonged to the ballet as the early twentieth century belonged to interpretive dance and it is difficult to dispel the impression of anachronism that may accompany this music juxtaposed with a more contemporary expressive language.

Music composed with electronically produced sounds provides the dancer with an unusually rich assortment of material, particularly for use in improvisational studies. The reasons why this music "works" for dance are not yet entirely apparent but one may speculate somewhat. First of all, the music written for electronic media, in its superficial aspect if not in conception, is usually quite primitive and easily grasped by the inexperienced listener. The musical gestures are more obvious because the tonal systems employed to manipulate them are less subtle than the traditional tonal system which represented some three hundred years of development. Secondly, the range of possibilities connected with the sounds themselves, unrestricted by the limitations of standard orchestral instruments, provides a background palette less restraining on the dancer's own sensibilities regarding phrasing and breathing. Some of our contemporary composers who write for instruments in such a way as to extend their previous limitations, for the same reasons also provide the dancer with excellent material. One may assume from the extraordinary success experienced with this kind of music used as motivation or support in improvisational situations that freshness of sound is an important stimulus.

Music for Classwork

What, then, are the ideals within practical reach of the dancer for fulfilling the daily musical need of the dance technique class? The music employed must be functional to its purpose; that is, simply, to support the metric and rhythmic structure of the exercises and to bend all its elements—melody, harmonic phrase, and rhythmic texture—to the physical support[2] of the dancer, relieving him of the necessity of constant counting. Although in the choice of music generally used for this purpose there is room for improvement, the dancer is limited to material recorded specially for this purpose or must rely on the tastes of his accompanist. What he can do is to learn enough about rhythm and music so that he is not in these matters subservient to his accompanist and, with enough knowledge at his command to evaluate his own needs, to make his musical selections freely from the vast supply of recorded music.

The dance technique class is not the place for the musical education of the dance student unless, of course, one considers music so simple and so exterior a medium of expression that it can be learned by some sort of osmotic process or else that the study of dance requires less than the undivided attention of the student. Neither is it advisable that the dance student approach the study of music as a musician might if his purpose is knowledge of music as a source of material for dance. If, however, he has first made an exhaustive study of rhythm, he will have opened an avenue of approach to music which is wholly relevant to his art and any subsequent study of music will be relevant and fruitful to himself as an artist.

The Dance-Music Form

By far the optimum situation for the creation of a dance-music form is one in which the choreographer and composer may work individually from a common motivation toward a common goal, the details being worked out bit by bit once that goal is mutually agreed upon. This goal, which could be motivated by the desire for a dramatic or theatrical effect, could also be a specific form, the telling of a story, the realization of a visual concept, or even a

2. The word *support* should not convey the impression of an ironbound structure inside which the dancer is forced to move in a certain way; rather, it means that which allows the dancer to move freely as well as accurately.

historical or literary subject. In any case, it is precisely this theatrical dimension that lends unity of conception and projective power to the whole without compromising either of its parts. The uniqueness of each artistic endeavor involving a correlation of music and dance must be increasingly realized. And one hopes that the practice of selecting music intended for some other time and purpose to go with a dance that is created here and now will fall into disuse.

Rhythm

Dance (in which category we can include all forms of organized physical movement) and music do not have the same rhythmic structure. The rhythmic structure of any piece of music depends upon the following:

1. Pitch organization; melody or melodic articulation
2. Harmonic rhythm—by which is meant the speed and extent of change from one harmonic grouping to another
3. Motivic development of rhythmic patterns
4. Miscellaneous considerations such as proportions, texture, physical limitations of instruments and instrumentalists

It is obvious that dance is not affected by most of these considerations, though it is affected immediately, or by close analogy, by those related to the organization of time. What music and dance do share, then, is the common need for a system for the organization of time comprehensible to and consistent with the physical and psychological nature of the human being. Such a system in music has been in the process of development and refinement for many hundreds of years and the notational system which has accompanied and kept pace with these developments has reached such a degree of efficiency and subtlety that it is possible to transcribe in it the time relationship and relative emphasis between two or more notes with absolute precision.

Is this system of organization, then, a tool which the dancer can afford to be without, or to understand only imperfectly? In this era of the development of nonliteral forms in dance, as the dancer increasingly looks to pure movement as a basic source of material, can he neglect the creative possibilities of one of the prime ingredients of movement expression?

The dancer has in the past found it convenient to draw upon some aspects of rhythmic relationships between dance and music. Had he not had this fruitful source from which to borrow, however primitively, an independent theory of rhythmic movement based on its own needs would surely have developed by this time. Those who are satisfied that dance and dance forms can aspire to nothing more than a choreographic imitation of the rhythmic patterns of a selected musical composition need not concern themselves with the type of study material recommended here. Others who cannot accept this as a final goal, or even as a valid practice, must select only the elements and materials of our musical sources necessary to begin to understand rhythmic movement, and, establishing these as a basis, proceed to other more significant explorations.

What is advocated here, then, is a less humdrum reliance on music to project what the dancer, by thorough rhythmic training, must assume as his responsibility, and a more imaginative insight into discovering deeper relationships when combining the two arts.

The following pages outline a suggested course of study for the nonmusician. It is based on premises supplied by the implicit and explicit definitions of materials culled from the general practice of musicians and composers from the middle of the seventeenth century through the end of the nineteenth century. This outline provides some basic definitions and an order of procedure for the mastering of fundamental rhythmic skills which must be supplemented and enlarged upon once the student has begun to grasp elementary principles and to experience their value through practical application. It is advisable that the course be taught initially by a thoroughly trained musician though it can ultimately be used also as a guide for the experienced dancer who is to teach a course in rhythmic fundamentals within the scope of a college curriculum.

Basic Terminology

A first or introductory session must be devoted to definitions of terms to be used during the course, the correct usage of which will be absolutely indispensable to the study of rhythm. A strict adherence to the conditions implied by the wording of the following definitions[3] should be emphasized throughout.

Pulse[4]—the regular recurrence of equal phenomena. We recognize as the pulse the first and strongest event of any metric grouping or measure.

Measure—the interval between two pulses.

Meter—a regular arithmetical division of the time interval between pulses.

Beat—the pulse or any of its main divisions as represented by the meter.

Subdivision—the division of any beat into smaller units.

Rhythm—any organization of strong and weak stresses. It will subsequently be clear that, to be communicable, rhythmic organization must be consistent with the properties of the specific meter through which it is expressed.

Tempo—the speed of the pulse.

Meter signature—numerical symbols by which we identify the

3. There is a tendency for standard dictionaries and reference works—musical dictionaries included—to confuse and liberally interchange some of the terms presented here in such a way as to make a logical approach to what is a purely logical system of organization utterly impossible. At their very best, the definitions of these terms will be too general in scope to impart an understanding of their specific meanings as they pertain to the abstract study of rhythm outlined here. For this reason, all definitions are supplied within the text and will be found to be clearer, more to the point, and at the same time not inconsistent with the more generally understood meanings of the words.

4. The definition and concept of pulse presented here will naturally broaden as the level of study becomes more advanced, and the various manipulations of the pulse beat, such as a retardation or acceleration of the pulse and changes of meter, which bring the pulse beats into more complex relations with each other, will then be readily understood.

metric structure of the measure (or measures) to which they refer and the type of note selected to represent each beat.

Dividing the pulse

Each student should be equipped with a hand drum; the instructor, also with a drum, will devise exercises based on the following:

1. Students should be able to produce a series of equally stressed pulse beats in any tempo set by the instructor.

2. Using a wide range of examples of different metric patterns in varying tempi, and without previously communicating the tempo, have the students pick out the pulse and determine the meter. (Examples may be confined to the practical meters from two to seven if preferred.)

3. Have students reproduce on their instruments examples given by the instructor. Strict attention must be given to tempo and the stressing of the first beat.

4. In a given tempo the students should perform any metric division requested by the instructor.

Notation

Students are provided with a chart of all note and rest symbols (whole notes and rests to thirty-second notes and rests inclusive) excluding the qualifying symbols such as the dot and tie. Discussion of the correct usage of the symbols should clearly emphasize the *relative* value of the symbols and their interdependence with the specific time signature in question. Good writing habits right from the beginning will be a strong technical asset to the student. All notation should be done in pencil (a soft, dark pencil is most convenient) so that inaccuracies may be immediately corrected. Particulars of placement, spacing, and design of the symbols must be thoroughly demonstrated. The procedure for "binding" or "beaming" eighth and sixteenth notes, etc., for visual clarity should be presented.

The goal of these exercises is to develop the ability to construct arithmetically accurate and legible measures with reference to any time signature. Numerous exercises should be completed to this end.

Simple Meters

1. Duple meter[5]: pattern of stresses—strong, weak. Exercises should consist of listening and performing, later notating. Always vary tempi and achieve the widest range of experience in notating by varying the unit of measure (i.e., 2/2, 2/4, 2/8). The student should accomplish unequivocal performance in any tempo achieved by the accurate accentuation of the stress pattern of a series of measures in duple meter. Teach standard conducting pattern.[6]

5. The concept of duple meter as a manifestation of the binary nature of the human body might merit some discussion. This binary nature creates the impulse to organize equal events in terms of alternation, such as left-right, tick-tock, click-clack. Triple meter can then be referred to as an intellectual extension of the organizational impulse.

6. In the manipulation of rhythmic problems, a metric norm appropriate to the situation must be maintained, preferably one that is controlled by the student. For the dancer beginning his studies in rhythm, conducting, or the arm motion representing a metric pattern, is the ideal norm for several reasons: 1) it is primarily a physical activity; 2) a relaxed and fluent conducting technique may serve as a key to rhythmically alive physical activity; 3) it supplies the student with an immediate method for projecting a rhythmic idea; 4) the movements themselves are easy to grasp and kinetically logical, thus insuring from the beginning a large degree of accuracy; and 5) technical proficiency in dance technique is not a prerequisite for the practice of conducting. A pianist, for example, may supply his own norm through counting aloud—a physical coordination, incidentally, which is unfortunately underrated for the instruction of beginning students. Counting out loud will in some situations and at some point finally take over for the dancer where conducting leaves off, and its advantage over counting "inwardly" (which is the ultimate goal for the establishing of a metric norm) is that, the auditory sense being uninvolved in either, the metric or rhythmic physical expression tends to remain critical and uninfluenced by physical difficulties and will more readily detect irregularities. It is for the same reason that the metric norm must be established *apart* from the actual physical problem—so that it is not easily bent to accommodate technical difficulties.

2. Triple meter: pattern of stresses—strong, weak, weaker. The exercises and goal will be the same as for duple meter. Teach standard conducting pattern.

Subdivision

Apply principles of duple and triple patterns of stress to simple subdivisions of any beat within the two simple meters. The bracketed triplet as a notational device may be introduced at this time or postponed until a more complete discussion of this principle can be undertaken. The first exercises in dictation should be given at this point, the tempo and metric unit to be indicated by the instructor.

Exercises should consist of sequences of four or multiples of four measures in various duple and triple meters of the students' invention and should be performed in class. A large variety of rhythmic patterns are now available to the student through the use of simple subdivisions and a balance must be maintained between the complications that a student may invent on paper and his ability to perform them accurately. It is in this type of endeavor that a student should be encouraged to expand his performance ability by means of his intellectual imagination. Exchange exercises and have each student both perform and conduct his own and other students' exercises.

The Upbeat, or Preparatory Beat

During his first conducting experience, the confusion and awkwardness experienced by the student in getting things started at the right time and in the right tempo will precipitate the proper climate for attacking this most elusively difficult problem of rhythmic communication—the upbeat. Whole volumes could be devoted to the various aspects of the preparatory beat (or beats) in music and analogies can be drawn with life situations in which, if the preparation be faulty, the execution cannot help but be faulty. While this is not the place to dwell on the ramifications of this concept, it should be immediately apparent to the dancer or to anyone involved in the development of physical facility that skill in this area will be most crucial in his or her performing and teaching experience. Being precisely an activity of mental and kinetic coordination, the act of conducting will provide the best training ground for the incorporation of this technique; indeed, conducting is not possible without it and, for a dancer, will specifically begin to develop the sense of preparation in time. Later, the dancer will transfer this sense to problems of breathing and moving and hopefully provide himself with an extra tool with which to analyze and correct the errors of his own students. The exact method of teaching the upbeat within the conducting patterns must be left to the individual instructor.

Quadruple Meter

Pattern of stresses—strong, weak, less strong, weaker; or—strong, weak, less strong, stronger; or—strong, less strong, weak, weaker. This is by far the most complex of all metric organisms. A fine awareness of the subtleties of quadruple meter can best be developed when the student has enough reading facility to study and listen with scores to many musical examples from the common practice period.

In the course of the usual exercises in listening, performing, taking dictation, and inventing rhythmic patterns within the new meter, the emphasis should be on the distinction between a subdivided measure of 2 (4 eighth notes) and an unsubdivided measure of 4 (4 quarter notes). The latter describes four real events with an inherent possibility of stress variation—especially concerning the second and fourth beats—and the former expresses two real events with subordinate or dependent material.

Compound meters

1. Six: pattern of stresses—*I*, 1, 3, *II*, 2, 4. For purposes of consistency and logic of approach, insist that the patterns of stress be strictly expressed so that any relaxation of the rule in practice,

particularly regarding the secondary[7] stresses, will be sensitively and knowledgeably handled (for example, in faster tempi and where a strong upbeat is involved).

2. Nine: pattern of stresses—*I*, 1, 4, *II*, 2, 5, *III*, 3, 6.

3. Twelve: pattern of stresses—*I*, 1, 5, *II*, 2, 6, *III*, 3, 7, *IV*, 4, 8. Have students write compositions in quadruple and sextuple meters, eight measures in length, including exploring the various methods of implementing the upbeat so that it emphasizes the motion to the pulse beat of the next measure.

The entire palette of exercises outlined in previous sections— listening, performing, and dictation—should be in continuous use throughout all class periods. Review also should be liberal.

Metrically Related Changes of Tempo

The students' technique must include the ability to handle the following problems (exercises in conducting and execution on the drum should be designed accordingly):

1. From a given tempo, change to a tempo twice as fast.

2. From a given tempo, change to a tempo half as fast.

3. The unit of measure remaining constant, change from duple to triple meter and the reverse.

Depending on individual ability, exercises modeled on the above might be extended to include more complexly related meters.

---

7. The term *compound meter* usually refers to those meters characterized by ternary divisions of the primary beats. Here *all* beats indicated by the meter signature will be considered as primary beats belonging to one of two groups—I or Ia—group I being distinguished by its higher relation to a simple meter. For convenience here, the Roman numerals will designate the first group in order of diminishing strength, and the Arabic numerals will designate the second group, also in order of diminishing strength. Although one may refer to group Ia as secondary metric stresses, it should be clear that they need not represent or be represented by actual rhythmic events that must be considered secondary. If this is consistently the case, however, it is possible that a simple meter, subdivided, will more accurately represent the rhythmic events.

Alternate and Simultaneous Expression of Duple and Triple Meters

Compare a measure of 3/4 subdivided (6 eighth notes) with a measure of 6/8.

Exercises:

1. Alternate in sequence—on drum or clapping (eighth note remains constant).

2. Excute one on drum, simultaneously counting the other out loud. (The word *and* here, as always, may represent the subdivision.) Reverse.

3. Conduct one while counting aloud the other. Reverse.

4. Go back and repeat all exercises articulating only the principal beats of the 3/4 measure and the first and fourth beats of the 6/8 measure. Compare results to a juxtaposition of a 2/4 with a 3/4 measure.

Exercises may be extended to include:

5. A drumstick in either hand, represent two against three in any given tempo.

6. The measure remaining constant, conduct in alternating sequence a two and a three.

Other Notational Symbols: Definitions and Usage

A *tie* is used to indicate a combined durational value of the two notes which it connects and is used in situations where no other expression of that value is possible. Such a situation occurs, for example, when a durational value extends across the bar-line. It is also used in cases where it will enhance visual clarity as compared with some other equally correct representation.
of the symbol which it qualifies by one-half.

A *dot* placed after the note-head increases the durational value of the symbol which it qualifies by one-half.

A *bracket* with a number placed above it referring to the number of equal units contained within the bracket indicates that the equal number of units occupies the space of the usual number of equal units occupying that space. For example, a space ordinarily occupied by two quarter notes may also be occupied by three quarter notes, bracketed, and the entire group is read as—3 quarter notes in the time of 2 quarter notes. This more primitive device is necessary in this example because we do not have in general usage a direct symbol to indicate a third part of a single beat.

Complex Meters

Measures containing five or more principal events generated by a single pulse will usually break down into simpler groups: five can be divided into two plus three or the reverse, seven into three plus two plus two, and so on. Each smaller group will be governed by its own metric pattern of stresses and the initial beat of each of these groups will relate back to the pulse as secondary and tertiary stresses, the hierarchy of related stresses being variable according to the specific situation.

As a project, have the student prepare and perform a selected piece of music written with two distinct rhythmic voices, using two hand drums of different pitch, each one representing a single voice.

The following pieces taken from the Bartok *Mikrokosmos*, volumes III, IV, and V are excellent material. The category designated as *professional*, although not to be attempted by students at this level, might serve to demonstrate what the capable professional dancer or dance educator should be expected to be able to handle.

Easy: Nos. 70, 78 (slowly), 99, 128 (easy-medium)

Medium: Nos. 78, 81, 115, 128

Difficult: Nos. 82, 88, 100, 113, 120

Professional: (medium) No. 139. (difficult) Nos. 124, 129, 133

If facilities are available, a short discussion of various percussion instruments, their characteristics and methods of being played, plus a possible final project incorporating their use, will provide students with still another aspect of rhythmic materials from which to draw upon subsequently in their own careers. Instruments should be divided into two main categories—those which are capable of sustaining sound (Such as cymbals, gongs, ratchets), and those that are capable only of articulating attacks. The project itself might consist of a composition for three or more players (any practical number of instruments may be used by each player) of at least twenty-four measures, which will be rehearsed and conducted by the composer and performed by classmates. An extensive discussion of the layout and clarity of the score will be necessary.

Analysis and Notation of Rhythmic Patterns in Speech

The following program of exercises, progressing in difficulty, is designed primarily to develop the "inner ear." They further provide an opportunity for practice in physical control by coordinating the spoken word with a metric or rhythmic pattern in the various ways described below.

1. Select words of three or more syllables and locate the principal accent, for example, *cu*linary, im*pa*tience, satis*fac*tion, organi*za*tion. While the instructor conducts any metric pattern, the student should pronounce the word with the accented syllable falling on the pulse or downbeat and the other syllables falling where they may. When this is accomplished easily, the instructor should go on to vary his tempi and to switch meters without warning. (It will be necessary in some cases to allow the student to vary the interval of his response to once every two or more measures.) Through the difficulties encountered in this practice, it will become evident to the student that in the case of words with extended upbeats, such as *organiza*tion, it will be necessary, in order to respond with consistent accuracy, that he also determine the exact durational value of the syllables contained in the upbeat. In this case, for example, the three syllables preceding the downbeat are equal in a moderate 4/4 measure to three sixteenths; hence, by subdividing the fourth beat into four, the student should be able to place the upbeat as well as the primary accent properly, and with this information more easily adjust to fluctuating tempi and changing meters.

Now the student must be able to conduct himself and others through the above exercises making certain that neither the voice nor the hand retards or accelerates the tempo to accommodate the other. Any lack of discipline in this area leads to poor rhythmic habits extremely difficult to break. Any vocal distortion must also be discouraged, as it may constitute an additional threat to the development of rhythmic control.

2. From the instructor's dictation, have the student notate the exact rhythmic pattern of a single word or a short phrase and indicate its precise placement in the measure. The instructor should accompany each word or phrase with a rhythmic pattern on the drum that clarifies, *not duplicates*, his intention. The student notates only the spoken word.

3. Have the student select a series of words, preferably a string of related nouns (such as the various pieces of furniture and accessories that one may find in the kitchen) with and without upbeats (which could be supplied at will by affixing the definite article *the*) and make a continuous setting for them with an instrumental accompaniment. Each unit should appear twice so that it can be performed antiphonally by the student and the class. The interval of accompaniment between words is the vehicle by which the meter and tempo is clarified, the interest and forward motion of the whole is sustained, and an adequate preparation for the spoken unit itself is given. The exercise should include at least one metric change. Some poetic distortion, consciously contrived, particularly where it adds something to the general spirit of the piece, is certainly permissible.

4. The next phase is the notation of simple sentences selected by the instructor. Allowing for small differences of inflection and quality of speech, the ultimate criterion for judging the success of any student's setting of a particular sentence is whether the student actually does most naturally recite the sentence as he has notated it. It is best to express the bulk of the rhythmic pattern in terms of a

single measure, the upbeat (or beats) occupying the necessary portion of the preceding measure.

An alternative final project that may be considered would be the dramatic setting of a short poem or piece of prose with instrumental accompaniment for several players and speaker.

Accent Displacement; Syncopation

Below are offered some brief definitions and comments intended to clarify the entire subject of syncopation. Syncopation will be most effectively understood at an advanced level when all the fundamentals of metric structure have been thoroughly absorbed and put into common practice.

Expressive accents. Any beat of any measure may be emphasized more than or instead of the pulse; likewise, any part of any beat may be emphasized more than or instead of its principal. This is to be regarded as an *atypical* stress in the context in which it occurs to insure its expressive power. Its consistent use as a *typical* stress within the broad framework of the measure will render it less effectual because it will force the listener or spectator to realign the measure according to what is manifestly the strong beat.

The shifting of a rhythmic pattern or group to a position in which the primary stress of the rhythmic pattern does not agree with the primary stress of the metric structure through which it is expressed is known as *syncopation*. Thus, if a simple group of 4 quarter notes in 4/4 begins on the second half of the first beat, thereby emphasizing not only that weak portion of the beat but every weak half of every beat in that measure, a real syncopation has been effected.

It may be easily seen, considering still the above example, that if the real, or metric pulse or some real stress is not also manifested along with the syncopated pattern or interspersed with it, the effect of the syncopation is diminished and soon lost as the observer tends to displace the group once more—back to its normal or most convenient metric position. The occasional omission of an expected strong beat or the unexpected prolongation of a weak beat may also be aptly considered to be syncopated effects.[8]

The presentation of all of the preceding material should occupy one half of a college semester or a minimum of fifteen class hours. The remainder of the semester should be devoted to the practical application of the acquired information to the special needs of the dancer or dance teacher. Though *practical*, this phase of the work should in no way be considered less rigorous in its demands upon the student in the area of technical precision. To this will be added the exacting process of learning through observation of the results achieved. To this end of successful application, it is obvious that only an instructor well versed and practiced in the foregoing studies —their principles, terminology, and concepts—can help his students toward the sound synthesis of information and practice necessary to keep the newly acquired knowledge fresh in the students' memory and imagination.

The class now might well be conducted in the spirit of a workshop, in which the key words will be experimentation, observation, and analysis. The following guide will provide the reader with some idea of the material that remains to be covered in order that a firm foundation be established for the use of rhythmic tools.

I. Movement practice and rhythmic analysis:
    A. All basic locomotor patterns
    B. All standard floor, barre, and center exercises
    C. Classic and traditional dance step patterns; optional—folk and social dance step patterns

II. Practice in drum accompaniment and study of accompanying techniques and principles. As a *basic* requirement, students should be able to accompany as well as rhythmically control through his accompaniment, all of the activities listed above under I.

8. In most cases when specifically applied to movement, these effects are better called *suspensions* and allow the word *syncopation* to refer to a rhythmic texture of longer duration.

III. Rhythmic direction as a part of classroom teaching technique:

    A. Students should be given an opportunity to direct group rhythmic activity through which they may broaden their experience in the lucid presentation of material, the establishment of a desired tempo, and the giving of a correct and helpful preparatory beat.

    B. Still in reference to the above, students must gain facility in projecting rhythmic ideas through the use of the voice and body, as well as with the drum, and learn to move rapidly from one to the other as the circumstances require.

    C. Tempo and rhythmic adjustments that become necessary because of the varying capacities and limitations dependent upon age and level of advancement of the groups taught is an important subject that must be investigated.

IV. Listening to music:

    A. Students should have some practice in identifying by ear the metric organization of selected musical compositions.[9]

    B. Listening to recordings with score in hand will provide the student with opportunities for direct experiences toward the understanding of metric and rhythmic organization in music.

V. Creative work; movement generated and developed from a rhythmic idea or concept; movement studies focusing on rhythmic balance and design; and, finally, the choreography of some small works with music.

---

9. Some allowances must be made here for differences in perception or interpretation, since the students have not been trained to take into account the subtle interaction between rhythm and harmony which is the special province of music. It is nevertheless true that students, at this point, should not mistake a measure of two for three, or three for four, even on first hearing.

Lighting for Dance

Some Philosophical Considerations

One basic approach to lighting contemporary dance stems from contemporary aesthetic philosophy which defines an art product as a time-space organization expressed directly in terms of an energy; for example, a painting (the art product) is an organization of color. Contemporary art places no demand upon the painter to produce a particular kind of organization, or to use a specific material. That the organization may represent marsh grass, or that the materials may be actual buttons does not contradict definition. There is no compulsion to picture objective or subjective reality. The art product is a painting if it constructs materials in such a way as to evoke an awareness in the spectator's color senses and through that awareness presents a "color-meaning."

Similarly, a dance is an organization of motion; and contemporary art places no demand on its organization or materials. It demands no literary narrative, no use of familiar movement patterns. A dance may present the birth, life, and death of impatience, or a dancer may ride a bicycle without violating a definition which predicates simply that the particular motional construction which evokes kinesthetic response is dance. The spectator views the organization of color, motion, sound (music), or mass (sculpture) and brings to the organization his own particular history of being.

By "history of being" I mean to imply much more than "experience"—not simply knowledge, but "way of life," unformulated environmental impingements, habit, total of exposure and physical and psychical results from this total. It is a man's unique history which gives to him (by way of his direct sensing of the energies involved) his unique insight into the content of a work of art, just as the artist's unique sensorium and history constructs it.[1]

In considering dance lighting one may refer to these philosophical tenets. The energy medium, whose organization creates the product, is light—light in any form, light from any source. The art product is lighted dance. The designer may use conventional stage lighting instruments or automotive headlights; he may elect simply to turn light on to begin and to turn it off to end, or he may choose to provide an indeterminate number of lighting changes without violating any precept. If his focus has been on the structuring of light toward that aesthetic end which the motion has projected, he has made a valid contribution to production.

Fundamentally the communication of dance is metakinetic, that is, the meaning of dance comes to the spectator through and beyond motion. Motion is "seen" by way of kinesthetic sensors, located in muscles, which "tell" us what moves when and how. These sensors frequently supply correlative data of attitude, emotion, and environment. They can give the sentient spectator the performer's pleasure or pain, not through symbolic, intellectual translation, but through direct, sympathetic muscular activity. (Specific motion is not equivalent to specific attitudes. We are all familiar with the circumstance in which the smile, symbolic of friendliness, may cover virulent animosity.) Through similar data transference, the muscles can tell the projected size, shape, and condition of space in which movement takes place. The spectator need only allow his

1. For a more detailed treatment of modern aesthetics, the reader may wish to explore the following: Rhys Carpenter, *The Esthetic Basis of Greek Art* (Bloomington: Indiana University Press, 1959); John Dewey, *Art as Experience* (New York: Minton, Balch & Co., 1934); Amedee Ozenfant, *Foundations of Modern Art* (New York: Dover, 1952); Stephen C. Pepper, *The Work of Art* (Bloomington: Indiana University Press, 1953); Frank Lloyd Wright, *Of Architecture* (New York: Duell, Sloan and Pearce, 1941).

eyes to feed his kinesthetic sensors to know the content of the motion of dance.

The eye is the receptor organ for many other senses. It is directly concerned with brightness and color, indirectly with balance, texture, duration, etc.[2]

Because the eye is the receptor organ for so much of our sensory data, light is a vital medium of sensation. The eye sees so much more than motion that every facet of lighting becomes an integral part of the total art impact of stage dance. The basic function of lighting is to make visible the *dance*, as opposed to the *dancer*. Each detail of lighting contributes to the visibility of the overtones of motion and to the statement of the lighted dance by way of light's aesthetic impact as well. Thus, light structure has meaning in itself. For example, a bright, white light makes a different aesthetic impact than a dim red light.

Form (the shape and condition of energy) has a meaning in and of itself. "A length of line, seen to be short, evokes a certain aesthetic action in man. A length of line, seen to be long, evokes a different action. Similarly a given number of lines of definite, diverse length will evoke different action with each different positional organization. So it is with planal values, with solids, with temporal aspects, with color, light, sound, motion, each organization having its own aesthetic value, producing a reality of its own."[3] Thus, the careful structure of light will augment the motional statement (as well as provide visibility) by way of its own aesthetics.

When form has no other purpose than its aesthetic value, the product is art. For example, the flashing of a red signal lantern on a highway at night, although reaching us by way of our senses and our history of being, is placed on that highway for the sole purpose of warning. The same signal lanterns, carried by dancers on

2. Wolfgang Von Buddenbrock, *The Senses* (Ann Arbor: University of Michigan Press, 1958).

3. Ruth Grauert, *The Dance Theatre of Alwin Nikolais* (theatre booklet of the Henry Street Playhouse, 1963).

stage, do not warn us away, but rather create for us a "light" meaning.[4]

The Procedure

In an effort to make tangible the intangible principles in which art is rooted, security-seeking educators have attempted to approximate the traditional, classical methods of a "sure" end and a series of "sure" steps toward that end. Most schools continue to attempt to define the art product in specific terms and in so doing support a logical formalization for production.

All kinds of schools retain to some degree this fixation. Most of the giants of modern dance, who developed their art image during the fomentation of the thirties, seem to have abandoned, in the pedagogical process, the procedures of creativity. Instead they elevate the specifics which they themselves created. Technique classes are built upon movement phrases derived from concert works. Specific motion, by intellectualization, is equated to specific idea. "New" ballets are constructed for the most part from such motion whose aesthetics is buried in technical study and in symbolic meaning. Such ballets do lack intended specific meaning for the uninitiated spectator, though he be sentiently honed.

Historically this is what we may expect. However, because we expect it, we need not accept it for ourselves, nor need we perpetuate it, for at the same time that modern aesthetic philosophy makes traditional methodology untenable, it gives us a sound basis from which to proceed. It recognizes that art (including that of lighting contemporary dance) is an open discipline, that it has no fixed limits, not even the limit of spectator approbation.

Art is founded ephemerally upon the artist's unique moment of insight. Each art procedure depends upon the aesthetic judgment of the artist. From an artist's unique germinal insight, a unique

4. Alwin Nikolais, in *Vaudeville of the Elements*, premiéred at the Guthrie Theatre, Minneapolis, December 1965.

series of decisions develops a unique end product. Each decision progresses to the next, relying on aesthetic judgment in order to remain sound.

In lighted dance the primary insight and structure is the choreographer's. It follows then that the light designer's first function is to view the work as a spectator, his entire attention focused on the aesthetic import of the choreographer's work. That the dance may be derivative or primary, symbolic or direct, nauseating or edifying has no bearing on his function. His job as a spectator is to sense the motion and structure as the choreographer presents it.

The designer's sentience in perceiving the dance's content is a primary aspect of the designer-as-spectator. He is no ordinary spectator. He needs to approach dance without prejudice since the validity of his design depends upon his ability to proceed upon what the dance presents. In viewing a unique work (and he must presume each to be such until proven otherwise), any sophistication would be an absurdity. To fulfill his function the designer must view the dance with innocence.

It is a difficult requirement for a designer-spectator to spectate without value judgment (since no mature being is without a sense of values) a balanced structure of what is and what is not worthy of his time. For a lighting designer, such evaluation must come prior to spectating for the purpose of designing. Once he elects to design lighting for a specific dance event, he may no longer judge the worth of the dance product; any value judgment becomes peripheral to his function since his lighting decisions depend upon his ability to allow idea to come freely from his perception through his body of knowledge into concrete reality.

The designer's history of being bears directly upon his ability to see without preconception. He needs to be able to see motion and to allow his motion sense to report. To allow shape, change, passage of time, accumulation, texture, space—all the multitude of structures that can speak—to report directly in order to bring the spectator a total report is no simple process. Such spectating requires practiced diligence. Much of our culture negates this direct sensing, and the designer will need to release his senses to override the strictures which our culture places on them.

From childhood we are taught to ignore with deliberation much of the energy structures in the world around us. This education is a necessary adjunct for survival. We cannot allow all motion to move us, all matter to shape us, all intensities and colors to sink deep into our heads, all sounds to vibrate within our beings: should we try it we soon become ill, disoriented, and one of the unsurviving.

On the other hand, art is a *special* structure *intended* to inhabit us, so that our orientation, controlled by art, is somehow changed. To produce this change art requires us to permit our senses to take in all of it without our usual protective curtain.

This state of sensing demands self-controls, distinguished from self-hypnosis in the fact that the latter encompasses everything. Those of us who know art in this way have been on many trips without hallucinatory drugs. And each time we come home with our lives enriched.

Light design should evolve from a dance as the designer perceives it. Since his concern is with the structuring of light to heighten the dance statement, his technical knowledge becomes secondary. As a spectator his inner vision must be free of such technical concern so that he may envision a germinal lighting situation. The designer's ability to envision lighted dance, free from the necessity to use stage lighting in its traditional terms, is as vital to his creative contribution as his ability to spectate freely.

Once he has founded his germinal idea, he needs to work with any available instruments, whether traditional or otherwise, that will make his idea manifest. As it is with the dance itself, so it is with lighting dance. Around a germinal idea, properly founded on a dance, all other contributory lighting decisions are made in accordance with aesthetic judgment.

An Approach to Technique

In spectating a dance for the purpose of creating a dance lighting design, one should allow the vision of space-time-light structures to be evoked by the space-time-motion organization of the dance. In a moment of insight the lighting designer envisions planes of light and shadow occurring in a specific time coordination with motional occurrence. This germinal insight can serve as a foundation for the whole lighting structure; it is the initial decision, the place to begin.

Careful notes, made by the designer after his first viewing, or stage use, dynamic values and changes, narrative overtones, and any other pertinent motional or nonmotional content will enable him to procede from this initial insight to the series of decisions resulting in an overall lighting design.

The obvious next step in the designing process is to translate lighting vision into practical mechanical terms. It is here that the designer's technical knowledge is called upon.

In dance, the word *technique* has come to mean certain motional structures which distinguish one dance artist from another. For example, Russian ballet technique and Graham technique are major designations that include not only technique but also realms of aesthetics. In fields where technology is highly developed (such as electronic sound or lighting), the differentiation between technique and aesthetics is complicated by orientation to mechanical requirements. An inevitable duality results when aesthetic values depend upon technical procedures. Electronic musicians may be trapped into composing and listening to their scores from a technical, rather than an aesthetic, viewpoint, so that the mechanical production and reproduction become major objectives in themselves.

Lighting designers are easily deluded by this mechanical orientation, because lighting is a traditional discipline. Many technical cul-de-sacs are imposed by the traditions and rules of usage of the dramatic stage. To operate in aesthetic accord with contemporary dance, the lighting designer should make all his technical decisions with reference to his initial insight; he should choose his instruments, their placement on stage, their alterations and temporal functions solely because they will produce what he had originally envisioned for the dance.

Just as contemporary choreographers create without concern for established dance aesthetics, so those who design for contemporary dance should function free from the dictates of lighting tradition. Such independence requires aesthetic conviction. Nikolais has blinded his audiences with lamps deliberately focused to do just that.[5] Rauschenberg swept them with naked light.[6] The instruments used have frequently been exposed to audience viewing,[7] not always as deliberate design in itself,[8] but simply because overall design allowed no other solution.[9] Although these lighting eccentricities violated long-standing customs of lighting design, the decision on instrument location and focus was based on aesthetics. The designer must feel free to make the final decision in such areas.

Instrumentation

An instrument of lighting design, in accordance with contemporary aesthetics, is defined as anything that gives light, shapes it, controls it, or colors it. This broad definition includes not only traditional stage lighting devices,[10] but also a huge variety of in-

5. Alwin Nikolais, *Prism*, 1956.

6. Rauschenberg for Cunningham's *Winterbranch.*

7. Nikolais, *Imago*, 1963

8. There are many instances where exposed instrumentation has become a means of bringing the audience into the reality of the stage mechanism, notably by Sean Kenny in *Oliver.*

9. On certain stages no good lighting for downstage areas is possible without exposing instruments in the auditorium or on the apron.

10. For data on theatrical equipment, or for information about technical terms used herein, refer to Stanley McCandless, *A Method of Lighting the Stage*, 4th ed. (New York: Theatre Arts Books, 1958), or to manufacturer's catalogs such as Kliegel Brothers.

novative light-giving articles. Among these are nonelectrical sources
—candles, kerosene lanterns, torches, propane burners, fireworks,
braziers; battery-powered sources—flashlights, lanterns, and special combinations contrived for particular use; specialized instruments—Christmas tree lights, projectors (motion, slide and opaque),
shadow boxes, all household and commercial electrical fixtures;
and auxiliary materials such as mirrors, additional lenses, plastics,
metallic foils, and kaleidoscopes. All of these devices have been used
in contemporary dance.[11]

The lighting designer's technical knowledge should include not
only a knowledge of electrical functions, or the existence of instruments. It must include the vital awareness of the aesthetic quality
and impact of the energy aspects of stage and auxiliary instrumentation. The qualitative difference between a candle and a Christmas
tree lamp, over and above the lumens they produce or how they
are ignited, the different visual energy qualities of a scoop and a
leko of equal wattage, are essential tools in the designer's creative
equipment. His inner eye must see behind his vision of lighted dance
to the devices which may produce his vision.

Most contemporary choreographers compose motion based upon
the physical and aesthetic abilities of dancers, shaping performance
to produce their motional ideas. Should a given performer be un-
able to produce the desired image, the choreographer has two obvious choices—he can modify his idea, or he can seek a dancer
who can move within his image. So it is with the lighting designer.
He can function with available materials, altering them and shaping
them to produce his vision, or he can seek new material that will
better serve his objectives.[12]

11. Nikolais's works are signal in their use of eccentric lighting devices
culminating with *Somniloquy* (1967) using battery-powered projectors, and
Première (1967) using both motion and slide projectors.

12. It has been my experience that equally good effects can result when
one is forced to substitute a variety of unlikely instruments for those originally intended.

The selection of instruments and color media structures the energy involved in the art of light design. Light may be further structured by the wattage of lamps and by dimmer control. Shutters, irises, cutouts, slides, and other shape-controlling devices give the design control of spatial elements as does the choice of instrument location and the focus of the beam of light.

Summary of Procedure

The first function of the lighting designer is to view the dance work as a designing spectator, after which he makes practical notes of design idea and time-space-motion structures pertinent to formulation of light idea.

These notes serve as the basis for discussion of the lighting plan with the choreographer. The total design, the relationship between motion and light, and the effect of lighting processes on the total production are clarified at this juncture.

Next, the designer surveys the actual stage facilities and its instrumentation and control and makes a plot or diagram locating, focusing, and connecting the instruments he selects to produce the design. Eccentric instrumentation is procured or constructed and included in this plot.

This plot contains the spatial elements of the light design by the location and focus of the instruments and the quality of the energy with which the design is produced by the instruments indicated.

At the same time the designer makes a chart which clarifies the temporal aspects of design showing when particular instruments will be introduced, changed, or dismissed.

Until this moment lighting has been cerebral. The design is on paper and has its only actual existence in the mind of the designer. His next step is to work with the stage technicians in the actual placement of instruments as indicated on his plot. It is important to the final production that the designer maintain his sentience and vision during this procedure, for inevitably changes in the projected designs dictated by practical necessity need to be made and may be resolved positively through his insight and vision.

After the stage is set, the dancers walk through the dance as the lighting designer instructs the technicians in the operation of the light play as outlined in the temporal chart. The stage manager makes accurate records of all technical operations, for the final production depends upon this record. Again, the designer maintains his open perceptiveness for much positive design opportunity presents itself during actual visualization of light and motion together.

A rechecking of all operations is made during a preperformance run-through in which all elements (motion, sound, costume, decor, lighting, all pertinent stage operation) are presented as in actual performance.

In the run-through the gap between the sentience and the brain must close once more. To know in the instant of happening what changes need to be made in intensity, color value, lighting angle, instrumentation, takes the trained spectator who, while he watches, knows in his senses what to do, and intuitively goes directly to technology to repair and refresh his image.

Dance, as a theater art performed for spectators to view, has been presented in silence (without music or other aural addition); it has been presented naked (without any vestige of costuming). However, the election of silence and nakedness is an artist act; just as the election to perform in no light except incidental environmental light is an aesthetic judgment. Each act must harmoniously contribute to create the whole act of theater dance.

APPENDICES
GLOSSARY
INDEX

Bibliography on Dance Heritage and Related Reading

Books

Anderson, Harold H., ed. *Creativity and Its Cultivation*. New York: Harper and Bros., 1959.

Arbeau, Thoinot. *Orchesography*. Translated by Cyril W. Beaumont. Brooklyn: Dance Horizons, 1967.

Armitage, Merle. *Dance Memoranda*. Edited by Erwin Corle. New York: Meredith Publishing Co., 1947.

————. *Martha Graham*. Los Angeles: L. R. Kistler, 1937.

Broer, Marian R. *Efficiency of Human Movement*. Philadelphia: W. B. Saunders, 1966.

Cage, John. *Notations*, New York: Something Else Press, 1967.

Cheney, Gay, and Strader, Janet. *Modern Dance*. Boston: Allyn and Bacon, 1969.

Cohen, Selma J., ed. *The Modern Dance: Seven Statements of Belief*. Middletown, Conn.: Wesleyan University Press, 1966.

Cunningham, Merce. *Changes: Notes on Choreography*. New York: Something Else Press, 1969.

Duncan, Isadora. *My Life*. New York: Liveright, 1927.

————. *The Art of the Dance*. Edited by Sheldon Cheney. New York: Theatre Arts, 1928.

Ellfeldt, Lois. *A Primer for Choreographers*. Palo Alto: National Press, 1967.

Gray, Miriam, ed. *Focus on Dance, V: Composition*. Washington: American Association for Health, Physical Education and Recreation, National Section on Dance, 1969.

Gruber, Howard E.; Terrell, Glenn; and Wertheimer, Michael, ed. *Contemporary Approaches to Creative Thinking*. New York: Atherton, 1962.

Hawkins, Alma. *Creating Through Dance*. New York: Prentice-Hall, 1964.

————. *Modern Dance in Higher Education*. New York: Columbia University Press, 1954.

Hayes, Elizabeth. *Dance Composition and Production for High Schools and Colleges*. New York: Ronald Press, 1955.

————. *Introduction to the Teaching of Dance*. New York: Ronald Press, 1964.

H'Doubler, Margaret N. *Dance: A Creative Art Experience*. New York: F. S. Crofts, 1940.

Hering, Doris, ed. *Twenty-Five Years of American Dance*. 2d ed. Madison: University of Wisconsin Press, 1957.

Horst, Louis. *Pre-Classic Dance Forms*. New York: Dance Horizons, 1969.

————, and Russell, Carroll. *Modern Dance Forms in Relation to the Other Modern Arts*. San Francisco: Impulse, 1961.

Humphrey, Doris. *The Art of Making Dances*. New York: Grove Press, 1962.

Jones, R. W., and De Haahn, M. *Modern Dance in Education*. New York: Columbia University Press, 1948.

Kinney, Troy, and Kinney, Margaret. *The Dance*. New York: Stokes, 1924.

Kirby, Michael, ed. *Happenings: An Illustrated Anthology*. New York: E. P. Dutton, 1965.

Kneller, George F. *The Art and Science of Creativity*. New York: Holt, Rinehart and Winston, 1965.

Laban, Rudolf. *Modern Educational Dance*. London: MacDonald and Evans, 1948.

————. *The Mastery of Movement*. London: MacDonald and Evans, 1950.

Langer, Susanne K. *Feeling and Form*. New York: Charles Scribner's Sons, 1953.

————, ed. *Reflections on Art*. Baltimore: Johns Hopkins Press, 1958.

Lippincott, Gertrude. *Dance Production*. Washington: American Association for Health, Physical Education, and Recreation, 1956.

Lippincott, Gertrude, ed. *Focus on Dance, I*. Washington: American Association for Health, Physical Education and Recreation, National Section on Dance, 1960.

Lloyd, Margaret. *The Borzoi Book of Modern Dance.* New York: Alfred A. Knopf, 1949.

McCandless, Stanley R. *A Method of Lighting the Stage.* 4th ed. New York: Theatre Arts, 1958.

McLuhan, J. Marshall, *Understanding Media: The Extensions of Man.* New York: McGraw-Hill, 1964.

Martin, John. *America Dancing.* Brooklyn: Dance Horizons, 1968.

_____. *The Dance: The Story of the Dance in Pictures and Text.* New York, Tudor, 1947.

_____. *Introduction to the Dance.* Brooklyn: Dance Horizons, 1967.

_____. *The Modern Dance.* Brooklyn: Dance Horizons, 1965.

_____. *Sybil Shearer.* Lithography by John H. Darby. Palatine, Ill.: M. Yoshimasu, Box 515, 1965.

Mettler, Barbara. *Materials of Dance as a Creative Art Activity.* Tucson, Ariz.: Mettler Studios, Box 4456, 1960.

Morgan, Barbara. *Martha Graham.* New York: Duell, Sloan and Pearce, 1941.

Pease, Esther E., ed. *Compilation of Dance Research, 1901–64.* Washington: American Association for Health, Physical Education and Recreation, National Section on Dance, 1964.

Radir, Ruth A. *Modern Dance for the Youth of America.* New York: Ronald Press, 1944.

Raths, Louis A.; Harmin, Merrill; and Simon, Sidney. *Values and Teaching.* Columbus, Ohio: Charles E. Merrill, 1966.

Reid, Louis A. "Beauty and Significance." In *Reflections on Art,* ed. Susanne K. Langer. Baltimore: Johns Hopkins Press, 1958.

Sachs, Curt. *The Commonwealth of Art.* Washington: U.S. Government Printing Office, 1950.

_____. *World History of the Dance.* New York: Norton, 1946.

St. Denis, Ruth. *An Unfinished Life.* New York: Harper, 1939.

Selden, Elizabeth. *The Dancer's Quest.* Berkeley: University of California Press, 1935.

Smith, Nancy W., ed. *Focus on Dance, IV: Dance as a Discipline.* Washington: American Association for Health, Physical Education and Recreation, National Section on Dance, 1967.

Sorell, Walter. *Hanya Holm: The Biography of an Artist.* Middletown, Conn.: Wesleyan University Press, 1969.

_____. *The Dance Through the Ages.* New York: Grosset and Dunlap, 1967.

Stern, Paul, "On the Problem of Artistic Form." In *Reflections on Art*, ed. Susanne K. Langer. Baltimore: Johns Hopkins Press, 1958.

Stewart, Virginia. *Modern Dance*. New York: Barnes and Noble, 1942.

Terry, Walter. *Invitation to Dance*. New York: A. S. Barnes, 1942.

Tompkins, Calvin. *The Bride and the Bachelors*. New York: Viking Press, 1965.

Turner, Margery J. *Dance Handbook*. Englewood Cliffs, N.J.: Prentice-Hall, 1959.

————. *Modern Dance for High School and College*. Englewood Cliffs, N.J.: Prentice-Hall, 1957.

Vullier, Gaston. *A History of Dancing from the Earliest Ages to Our Own Times*. New York: Appleton-Century-Crofts, 1898.

Wigman, Mary. *The Language of Dance*. Translated by Walter Sorell. Middletown, Conn.: Wesleyan University Press, 1966.

Winearls, Jane. *Modern Dance: The Jooss-Leeder Method*. London: Adam and Charles Black, 1958.

Wotten, Betty Jane, ed. *Focus on Dance, III*. Washington: American Association for Health, Physical Education and Recreation, National Section on Dance, 1965.

————. *Focus on Dance, II: An Inter-disciplinary Search for Meaning in Movement*. Washington: American Association for Health, Physical Education and Recreation, National Section on Dance, 1962.

Articles

Bowers, Faubian. "Music to my Ears." *Saturday Review* 44 (Feb. 25, 1961): 36.

"Close-up of Modern Dance Today: The Non-Objective Choreographers." *Dance Magazine* 31 (Nov. 1957): 20–23.

"Close-up of Modern Dance Today: The Private Teacher." *Dance Magazine* 31 (Dec. 1957): 41–45.

"Close-up of Modern Dance Today: Symposium." *Dance Magazine* 32 (March 1958): 38–41.

"Close-up of Modern Dance Today: Symposium, Part II." *Dance Magazine* 32 (April 1958): 44–45.

Cohen, Selma J. "Avant-garde Choreography." *Criticism* 3, no. 1 (Winter 1961): 16–35.

Eiten, George. "Modern Dance and the Non-Verbal." *Dance Observer* 18, no. 8 (Oct. 1951): 116–17.

Fatt, Amelia. "Murray Louis in St. Louis: An Adventurous Three Week School Experiment." *Dance Magazine* 42 (March 1968): 58–64.

Goodman, Saul. "Biographical Sketch" (Paul Taylor). *Dance Magazine* 33 (June 1959): 48–49.

Hartley, Russell. "Parades and Changes, Scandal and Delight." *Dance Magazine* 39 (Oct. 1965): 50–51.

Hawkins, Erick. "Erick Hawkins Addresses a New-to-Dance Audience." *Dance Magazine* 41 (June 1967): 40–44.

Hering, Doris. "American Dance, A Growing Up." *Dance Magazine* 29 (July 1955): 22–27.

_____. "Punctuation of Personalities: American Modern Dance in the 1950's." *Musical America* 80 (Feb. 1960): 30–31.

_____. "Who Knows How I Appear?" *Dance Magazine* 37 (Nov. 1963): 46–47.

Langer, Susanne K. "The Dynamic Image: Some Philosophical Reflections on Dance." *Dance Observer* 23, no 6 (June–July 1956): 85–87.

Loftis, Norman J. "Choreography of the Object" (Cunningham). *Craft Horizons* 29 (March 1969): 10–13.

Louis, Murray. "Dear Alwin . . . From Murray Louis." *Dance Magazine* 43 (May and June 1969): 44–45, 83–84.

Marks, Marcia. "Scenes from an Unreachable World." *Dance Magazine* 44 (March 1970): 30–33.

Nikolais, Alwin. "Basic Dance and Sensory Perception." *Dance Observer* 31, no. 1 (January 1964): 6–8.

_____. "Total Theatre Environment." *Craft Horizons* 28 (May 1968): 14–17.

Rizzo, Francis, ed. "Globolink's Friend" (interview with Nikolais). *Opera News* 34, no. 8 (Dec. 20, 1969): 17.

Sorell, Walter. "Close-up of Modern Dance Today: The Henry Street Playhouse." *Dance Magazine* 32 (Jan. 1958): 48–52.

Terry, Walter. "Dances of and by Youth." *Saturday Review* 50 (Dec. 1967): 36.

_____. New Dance Age." *Etude* 74 (Nov. 1956): 17.

_____. "The Sunbeam Will Outlast Us All." *Saturday Review* 53 (Feb. 7, 1970): 42.

Turner, Margery J. "A Study of Modern Dance in Relation to Communication, Choreographic Structure, and Elements of Composition." *Research Quarterly of the American Association for Health, Physical Education and Recreation* 34, no. 2 (May 1963): 219–27.

—————. "Non-literal Modern Dance—Its Nature, Forms and Means of Communication." *Research Quarterly of the American Association for Health, Physical Education and Recreation* 36, no. 1 (March 1965): 86–96.

Periodical Issues

Entire issues of the periodicals listed below are devoted to topics that will be of interest to the reader.

ARTS IN SOCIETY

Vol. 6, no. 2 (1969) *Confrontation Between Art and Technology*
Vol. 7, no. 1 (1970) *Sounds and Events of Today's Music*

BALLET REVIEW

Vol. 1, no. 4 (1966) [Merce Cunningham]
Vol. 1, no. 6 (1967) [experimental dancers]
Vol. 2, no. 1 (1967) [Paul Taylor]
Vol. 2, no. 2 (1968) [chance dance]
Vol. 2, no. 4 (1968) [mixed media]
Vol. 2, no. 5 (1969) [avant-garde dancers]
Vol. 3, no. 2 (1969) [Kostelanetz on Cunningham]

DANCE PERSPECTIVES

No. 16 (1963) *Composer/Choreographer*
No. 28 (1966) *In Search of Design*
No. 30 (1967) *Cine Dance*
No. 34 (1967) *Merce Cunningham*
No. 38 (1969) *Dancer's Notes*
No. 41 (1970) *The Shapes of Space*

DANCE SCOPE

Vol. 1, no. 1 (Winter 1965) [experimental choreographers]
Vol. 1, no. 2 (Spring 1965) [contemporary works]
Vol. 2, no. 1 (Fall 1965) [contemporary and experimental dancers]
Vol. 4, no. 2 (Spring 1970) [Twyla Tharp]

IMPULSE

(1953) *Dance in Education*
(1961) *The Dancer as a Person*

(1962) *Audience for Dance*
(1963–1964) *International Exchange in Dance*
(1965) *Dance and Education Now*

Dance Periodicals and Reference Sources

American Association for Health, Physical Education, and Recreation, Dance Division, Publishes the *Journal of Health, Physical Education and Recreation* and the *Research Quarterly*. 1201 Sixteenth Street, N.W., Washington, D.C. 20036.

Beaumont, Cyril W., ed. *A Bibliography of Dancing*. London: The Dancing Times, 1929.

Belknap, S. Y. *Guide to Dance Periodicals*, 7 vols. Gainesville: University of Florida Press, 1931–59.

Dance Magazine (monthly). 268 West Forty-seventh Street, New York, New York 10036.

Dance News (monthly). 119 West Fifty-seventh Street, New York, New York 10019.

Dance Observer. Discontinued after 1964.

Dance Perspectives (quarterly). 29 East Ninth Street, New York, New York 10003.

Dance Scope (semiannual). Published by American Dance Guild. 124–16 Eighty-fourth Road, Kew Gardens, New York 11415.

Impulse (annual). 160 Palo Alto Avenue, San Francisco, California 94114. Discontinued after 1970.

Magriel, Paul D., ed. *A Bibliography of Dancing*. New York: H. W. Wilson, 1936. 4th cumulated supplement 1936–40. 1941.

New York Times. Arts section; dance critic reviews.

Dance Films and
Film Distributors

The following films are all 16 mm., professional, and noninstructional in type. Distributor key follows listing.

Modern Dance Films

A DANCER'S WORLD. CF, DF. 30 mins. Black and white. Sound.
Martha Graham discusses the development of a dancer. Illustrations from the Graham company interwoven.

AIR FOR THE G STRING. 1949. DF, Todd. 10 mins. Black and white. Sound.
Bach interpretation by Doris Humphrey.

ALVIN AILEY DANCE THEATRE. 1962. WCBS. Black and white. Sound.
Roots of the Blues and *Creation of the World.*

AMERICAN DANCE THEATER: POEM. 1965. WCBS. Black and white. Sound.
Choreographed by Sophie Maslow, based on Ferlinghetti's poem "Autobiography." Discussion with Maslow.

APPALACHIAN SPRING. CF, DF, RF, Todd. 31 mins. Black and white. Sound. Martha Graham Company.

AS I LAY DYING. 1965. WCBS. Black and white. Sound.
Portions of Valerie Bettis's dance drama of William Faulkner's work of the same name.

A TIME TO DANCE. (Series of 9 programs moderated by Martha Myers.) 1959. NETC. 29 mins. each. Black and white. Sound.
1. Introduces three dance forms—modern, ballet, ethnic. Differences are illustrated by Maria Tallchief, Andre Eglevsky, Nora Kaye, Geoffrey Holder, José Limon.
2. Classical ballet—basic principles by Eglevsky and Tallchief.
3. Invention in dance—Nikolais and company.
4. A choreographer at work— John Butler in use of rhythm, space and theme.

5. The language of dance—José Limon explains the language of movement and basic element of human emotion.

6. Ethnic dance—round trip to Trinidad with Geoffrey Holder and Carmen de Lavallade.

7. Dance as a reflection of our times—Herbert Ross and group in *Caprichos* and excerpt from *Paeon.*

8. Great performance in dance—rare film samples of outstanding dancers, including Pavlova, Irene and Vernon Castle, Argentinita, and performance by Frederick Franklin and Alexandra Danilova. Walter Terry discusses choreography and performance relationships.

9. Modern ballet—Anthony Tudor, choreographer, and dancers Nora Kaye and Hugh Laing. Tudor discusses changes in form beginning in 1940s. *Pillar of Fire* performed.

DESPERATE HEART, THE. 1951. BF, FSU, Todd. 11 mins. Color. Sound.
Valerie Bettis's solo choreography based on a poem by John Malcolm Brinnin.

EVOLUTION OF THE DANCE. Todd. 10 mins. Black and white. Silent.
The Denishawn Company of 1918 in *Curios of the Dance*, done for a newsreel camera.

FIFTY YEARS OF DANCE. 1964. WCBS. Black and white. Sound.
Ruth St. Denis and Ted Shawn reminisce with Walter Terry.

ILLUMINATIONS. 1966. WCBS. Black and white. Sound.
Norman Walker's choreography to Benjamin Britten's music with text from the collection of poetry of Arthur Rimbaud.

INTEGRATION OF DANCE AND DRAMA. PM. 12 mins. Color. Silent.
Directed by Charlotte Perry and demonstrated by Harriette Ann Gray and Barney Brown.

LAMENT. CF, DF, Todd. 20 mins. Black and white. Sound.
Choreography by Doris Humphrey, based on a poem by Garcia Lorca and danced by José Limon, Letitia Ide, and Ellen Love.

LAMENTATION. 1943. DF. 10 mins. Color. Sound.
John Martin introduces the film and speaks about modern dance as a form of expression.

MERCE CUNNINGHAM. 1967. Cunningham. Color. Sound.

MOOR'S PAVANE. 1950. FSU, MSU, Todd. Black and white and color. 15 mins. Sound.
José Limon presents the study of Othello. Also performing are Betty Jones, Lucas Hoving, Ruth Currier.

MURRAY LOUIS. 1971. CHM. Color. Sound.

A series of fine films dealing with dance as an art form.

NIGHT JOURNEY. DF, RF. 30 mins. Black and white. Sound.

Martha Graham Company, based on Oedipus legend. Dancers include Bertram Ross, Paul Taylor, and Helen McGehee.

NEGRO SPIRITUALS. 1927. CF, DF. 17 mins. Black and white. Sound.

Helen Tamiris dances a suite of five solos. Interesting for historical study.

PAUL TAYLOR. WCBS. Repertory Dance Workshop Films.

PAUL TAYLOR, AN ARTIST AND HIS WORK. 1968. Harris. Color. Sound.

ROOMS. 1970. WCBS. Black and white. Sound. Choreographed by Anna Sokolow.

RUTH ST. DENIS AND TED SHAWN. EB. 28 mins. Black and white. Sound.

St. Denis's *Incense* and *White Nautch* and Shawn's *Japanese Warrior*. Of interest historically. Includes interview of the dancers.

SYBIL SHEARER. 1956. British Film Institute. Color. Sound.

Solo dances from a Carnegie Hall concert. From the *American Modern Dance* exhibit. The National Film Theatre of the British Film Institute.

THREE BY MARTHA GRAHAM. Graham. Color. Sound.

Seraphic Dialogue, *A Cortege of Eagles*, and *Acrobats of God*.

THREE CHOREOGRAPHERS. 1959. WCBS. Black and white. Sound.

Sokolow, Hamilton, Moncion.

TODAY'S DANCER. 1965. WCBS. Black and white. Sound.

Development of four hundred years of dance. Dancers are Michael Maule, Rochelle Zide, Pamela Ladimer, and Tony Catanzaro, with Walter Terry as guest.

YOUNG DANCERS. 1961. WCBS. Black and white. Sound.

Filmed from the High School of the Performing Arts.

Avant-garde Dance Films

ALWIN NIKOLAIS. WCBS. Repertory Dance Workshop Films.

CLINIC OF STUMBLE. 1950. C16. 16 mins. Black and white. Sound.

Experimental multi-exposure film. Choreography by Marian Van Tuyl. Film by Sidney Peterson.

COACH WITH THE SIX INSIDES. 1964. WCBS. Black and white. Sound.

Excerpts from Jean Erdman's dance drama version of James Joyce's *Finnegans Wake*.

DANCE CHROMATIC. 1949. C16. 7 mins. Color. Sound.

Experimental film by Ed Emschwiller. A fusion of dance, abstract painting, and percussion score.

FUSION. 1967. C16. Color. Sound.

Ed Emschwiller on Nikolais's dance.

HORROR DREAM. C16. 10 mins. Color. Sound.

Marian Van Tuyl's choreography of a dancer's anxiety preceding performance. Music by John Cage.

LIMBO. 1968. WCBS. 30 mins. Color. Sound.

Nikolais choreographs for the electronic medium.

MURRAY LOUIS. WCBS. Repertory Dance Workshop Films.

NIGHT IS A SORCERESS. 1963. AFC. 20 mins. Black and white. Sound.

Dramatic theater piece by the San Francisco Contemporary Dancers with music by George Auric.

RITUAL IN TRANSFIGURED TIME. 1946. W. 16 mins. Black and white. Silent.

Maya Deren's chorio-cinema film. Created in a vein similar to dance.

STUDY IN CHOREOGRAPHY FOR CAMERA. C16. 4 mins. Black and white. Silent.

Maya Deren's cine-dance with intermittent solos by Talley Beatty.

TOTEM. 1965. C16, FMC. 16 mins. Color. Sound.

Ed Emschwiller's cinematic treatment of Alwin Nikolais's *Totem*. Features Murray Louis and Gladys Bailin and others.

Film Distributors[1]

AF, Academy Films, 1145 N. Las Palmas, Hollywood, California 70000.

AFC, Audio Film Classics, 10 Fiske Place, Mt. Vernon, N.Y. 10550.

BF, Bailey Films, Inc., 6509 De Longpre Avenue, Hollywood, California 70000.

Barbara Mettler Studios, Box 4456, University Station, Tucson, Arizona 85700.

CA, Cinema Art, 1725 Washington Street, San Francisco, California 94109.

C16, Cinema 16, 175 Lexington Avenue, New York, N.Y. 10016.

1. Adapted from "Directory of Dance Films," *Dance Magazine* 39, no. 9 (Sept. 1965): 60–76, 88–90.

CF, Contemporary Films, Inc., 267 W. 25th Street, New York, N.Y. 10001, or 614 Davis Street, Evanston, Illinois 60201.

CHM, Chimera Foundation for Dance, Inc., 344 W. 36th Street, New York, N.Y. 10018.

Columbia, Columbia Broadcasting Studios, 51 W. 52nd Street, New York, N.Y. 10019.

Cor, Coronet Films, 65 E. South Water Street, Chicago, Illinois 60601.

Cunningham, The Cunningham Foundation, 75 E. 55th Street, New York, N.Y. 10022.

DF, Dance Films Incorporated, 130 W. 57th Street, New York, N.Y. 10019, or 614 Davis Street, Evanston, Illinois 60201.

EB, Encyclopedia Britannica Films, Inc., 1150 Wilmette Avenue, Wilmette, Illinois 60091, or 5625 Hollywood Blvd., Hollywood, California 90028.

FI, Films, Inc., 1150 Wilmette Avenue, Wilmette, Illinois 60091.

FMC, Film Maker's Cooperative, 414 Park Avenue South, New York, N.Y. 10016.

FSU, Florida State University, Audio Visual Center, Tallahassee, Florida 32301.

Graham, Martha Graham Center, 316 E. 63rd, New York, N.Y. 10021.

Harris, Harris Communications, P.O. Box 287, Lenox Hill Station, New York, N.Y. 10021.

MSU, Michigan State University, Audio Visual Center, East Lansing, Michigan 48823.

MMA, Museum of Modern Art Film Library, 11 West 53rd Street, New York, N.Y. 10019.

NETC, National Educational Television Center, 2320 Washtenaw Avenue, Ann Arbor, Michigan.

NFS, Net Film Service, Audio Visual Center, Indiana University, Bloomington, Indiana 47401.

New York Dance Film Society, 633 Ninth Avenue, New York, N.Y. 10036.

New York Public Library, Donnell Branch, 20 W. 53rd Street, New York, N.Y. 10019.

PM, Perry-Mansfield Motion Pictures, Steamboat Springs, Colorado 80477.

RF, Rembrandt Film Library, 267 W. 25th Street, Dept. D, New York, N.Y. 10001.

Thomas Bouchard, Stonybrook Road West, Brewster, Cape Cod, Massachusetts 02631.

Todd, Todd Film Collection, 25 Barrow Street, New York, N.Y. 10014.
University of Washington, Audio Visual Service, Seattle, Washington, 98100.
WCBS, WCBS-TV, 51 W. 52nd Street, New York, N.Y. 10019.
William Skipper Productions, 53 Semmes Avenue, Mobile, Alabama 36600.

Sources of Recorded Music

Collections

AFRO-AMERICAN DRUMS. Folkways P502CD.

COMPOSITION FOR SYNTHESIZER. Arel, Davidovsky, ElDabh, Luening, Ussachevsky. Columbia-Princeton Electronics Center MS 6566.

CONCERT JAZZ. Sauter-Finnegan Orchestra. Victor 1051.

LUTE MUSIC FROM ROYAL COURTS OF EUROPE. Julius Bream. Victor LSC 2924.

MUSIC FOR VOICE AND GUITAR. Julius Bream. Victor LM 2718.

MUSIC OF SOUTHEAST ASIA. Folkways 4423.

OUTSTANDING JAZZ COMPOSITIONS OF THE TWENTIETH CENTURY. Columbia C2S–831.

Individual Composers

BARTOK, BELA

Bagatelles Op. 6, Bartok 918

Mikrokosmos, Vox, SVBX 5425

Quartets, Columbia, D3S–717

BERG, ALBAN

Lyric Suite for String Quartet, Columbia, M2S–620

BOULEZ, PIERRE

Le Marteau Sans Maitre, Westminster, XWN 18746

CAGE, JOHN

Indeterminacy, Folkways 3704

Sonatas and Interludes for Prepared Piano, Composers Recordings, Inc. 199

Fontana Mix, Turnabout, 34046

CHAVEZ, CARLOS

Toccata for Percussion, Capitol P–8299

COWELL, HENRY
Piano Music, Folkways 3349

DALLAPICCOLA, LUIGI
Variazoni per Orchestra, Louisville, 545–8

DEBUSSY, CLAUDE
Preludes for Piano, Angel 35249
Images Pour Piano, Angel 35065

FALLA, MANUEL DE
Concerto in D for Harpsichord, Flute, Oboe, Clarinet, Violin and Cello, Decca (7) 10108

FELDMAN, MORTON
New Directions in Music, Columbia ML5403
Out of "Last Pieces (1962)," Columbia ML613–3

HARRIS, ROY
Elegy and Dance, Composers Recordings, Inc. 140
Sonata for Violin and Piano, Columbia ML 4842
Trio, University of Oklahoma, 1.

PARTCH, HARRY
Music of Harry Partch, Composers Recordings, Inc. 193

PERLE, GEORGE
Rhapsody for Orchestra, Louisville 545–9

RICHTER, MARGA
Piano Music for Children by Modern Composers (Hindemith, Hovanhess, Surinoch, Toch), MGM EL 381

RUGGLES, CARL
Evocations; *Lilacs*; *Portals*, Columbia ML 4986

SATIE, ERIK
Piano Music of Erik Satie, MGM E3154

SCHOENBERG, ARNOLD
Serenade for Septet and Baritone Opus 24, Columbia ML 4737

SESSIONS, ROGER
Black Maskers: Suite, Mercury 90423

STOCKHAUSEN, KARLHEINZ
Gesang der Junglinge, Deutsche Grammophon Gesellschaft – 138811

STRAVINSKY, IGOR
Agon, Westminster 9–600
L'Histoire de Soldat, Everest 3017
Symphony for Wind Instruments, London 6225
Three Pieces for Clarinet, Decca 9570

VARESE, EDGARD

Deserts (1954); *Arcana* (1927); *Offrandes* (1922), Columbia MS 6362

Poeme Electronique; *Hyperprism*, Columbia MS 6146

WEBERN, ANTON

Five Movements for String Quartet, Opus 5, Columbia MS 6103

Recorded Music for Teaching

COLMAN, JOHN

Music for Contemporary Dance, Hoctor 3046

GILBERT, PIA

Music for the Modern Dance, Hoctor 4015

LOHOEFER, EVELYN

Music for Modern Dance, Volume I, Dean MM–47

LUBIN, ERNEST

Music for Contemporary Dance, S & R Records 406

MCCOSH, CAMERON

Music for Modern Dance, Hoctor 3053

MALAMENT, SARAH

Improvisations for Modern Dance, Volumes I, II, Available from composer, 3215 Netherland Avenue, New York, N.Y. 10063

MILLER, FREDA

Accompaniment for Dance Technique, Second and Third Albums for Dance, Music for Rhythms and Dance, Department J., Box 383, Northport, Long Island, New York

Sources on Lighting and Lighting Equipment

Articles on Lighting Dance

Benke, Marjorie. "Painting the Stage Set with Light." *Design* 54 (Dec. 1952): 66.

"Electronics Lights the Stage." *Popular Science Monthly* 151 (Aug. 1947): 106–07.

Goodman, Saul. "Meet Jean Rosenthal." *Dance Magazine* 36 (Feb. 1962): 19–23.

Izenour, George C. "Revolution in Light: Electronic Control Console." *Theatre Arts* 31 (Oct. 1947): 73–75.

Jones, Robert E. "Light and Shadow." *Theatre Arts* 25 (Feb. 1941): 131–39.

Rosenthal, Jean. "Jean Rosenthal on Lighting Design as a Major Element of Dance Presentation." *New York Times* (July 21, 1963), II, p. 6:1.

Skelton, Tom. "Handbook of Dance Stagecraft." *Dance Magazine* 29–31 (October 1955–March 1957).

————. "Staging the Recital: Lighting Effects." *Dance Magazine* 31 (March 1957): 82–84.

Sources of Lighting Equipment

Century Lighting, 521 West Forty-third Street, New York, New York 10036

Kliegel Brothers, 321 West Fiftieth Street, New York, New York 10019

Glossary

Abstract dance: Dance which has in itself essential qualities for communicating without literal reference to the source of the idea; nonrepresentational dance

Choreography: The art and craft of inventing and composing dances

Contrast: Relative variance of two or more choreographic factors

Creativity: A process of invention according to one's concepts and unique abilities

Dramatic: Employing the form or style of the drama

Element: A component or constituent part of a whole

Factor: An element contributing to a specific result

Imagery: Formation of images, figures, associations

Immediacy: Urgency, a sense of feeling or idea related to the instant

Indeterminacy: Process of creating art that eliminates the imagination, taste, and judgment of the artist as the controlling force of the work

Kinesthetic: The type of sensory experience derived from the sense organs in the muscles, tendons, and joints when they are stimulated by bodily movement

Kinetic: Of or pertaining to motion with potential, such as kinetic energy: dynamic interplay of forces related to changing motion

Leko: An instrument with a reflector double lens system to intensify light

Literal: True to fact, without exaggeration or inaccuracy, strict in meaning and interpretation, message bound

Motion: That which results from the process of moving

Movement design: Movement that has recognizable lines of action

Movement imagery: Formation of movement images as a result of or in response to feeling; the images remembered as a result of moving or seeing movement

Movement quality: Distinguishing character or nature of movement

Organic dance: Dance which develops uniquely from a central core or source

Principle: Method of formation, operation, or procedure; guide to the realization of the desired product

Psychological: That dimension of a human being beyond the physical fact itself; the human soul, spirit, or mental faculties

Realism: Treatment of a subject with fidelity to nature or to real life

Scoop: An unlensed lamp

Space: An expanse extending in all directions

Style: A particular, distinctive, or characteristic mode of action

Symbolism: Communication through the use of symbols that represent or suggest ideas or subjects

Technique: Skill in dance performance

Time: Relative tempo, duration, and intensity of movement

Unity: Integration, oneness

Variety: Contrasts in tension and forces of movement factors such as space, time, range, dimension, movement quality

Vehicle of expression: The specific means of communication

Index